JASPER RIDGE
A STANFORD SANCTUARY

AUTHORS

BARBARA BOCEK NONA CHIARIELLO PAUL EHRLICH
HAROLD A. MOONEY JOHN H. THOMAS PETER M. VITOUSEK

PHOTOGRAPHERS

CHARLES COMFORT PETER LATOURRETTE JOEL SIMON

EDITOR

SUSAN WELS

STANFORD ALUMNI ASSOCIATION
STANFORD, CALIFORNIA

Jasper Ridge
A Stanford Sanctuary

*To the volunteers and
to Herb Dengler, who, enchanted by Jasper Ridge since 1917,
has taught us all*

Library of Congress Catalog Card Number 90-71113
ISBN 0-916318-43-5

First Edition
Printed in Hong Kong

CONTENTS

Entryway to Jasper Ridge

PREFACE

Stanford's extraordinary good fortune in having its own biological preserve, on land contiguous with its campus, flows from a very special piece of original wisdom: the decision of Senator Stanford to forbid the Trustees to sell any of the University's endowment lands.

To appreciate the power of this successor-denying ordinance, it is necessary only to drive along Route 101. As you look out the window to the west, you see the near ridges of the foothills. How few of them have escaped development; indeed, Stanford's hill lands are a welcome relief from this pattern. When you reach campus, you see behind the first foothills some more distant, impressively wooded elevations. These belong to the Jasper Ridge Biological Preserve.

Jasper Ridge is undeveloped today because foresighted provisions, even beyond the Senator's wise dictum, were made for its protection. Throughout the 1960s, we believed that its status was under serious threat. The Army Corps of Engineers had proposed a new flood control structure in the San Francisquito Creek that would have destroyed part of the habitat. At the same time, controversy raged over the routing of power to the Stanford Linear Accelerator Center (SLAC).

We biologists were told that the business office had development plans for the Ridge, whose status as a reserve was, at that time, somewhat ambiguous.

To secure its future, we persuaded the Administration to emphasize the Ridge's value as a biological resource when mounting the argument to turn away the Corps, to adopt a power routing scheme for SLAC that would spare the top of the Ridge, and to resist development and leave the Committee on Green Foothills satisfied. This was done, and Jasper Ridge emerged from these struggles with a firm commitment from the University for its preservation.

Later, this enhanced status made it possible to add Searsville Lake Park and the riparian areas adjoining it to the Preserve, and then to fence all public borders. These two moves engendered some controversy, which I remember all too well because it began while I was chairman of the Department of Biological Sciences and continued during Norm Wessells' term.

First, we had to deal with the people who had regarded the Searsville Lake "beach" as a favorite mid-Peninsula spot.

The ultimate redesignation of the lake was another source of controversy. Then began the task of negotiating with several local trail-riding groups who had become accustomed to special access to Stanford lands; some of the trails led over Jasper Ridge. One group, which called themselves "The Shack Riders"—this group included some particularly influential Stanford alumni and friends—had built a commodious "shack" on the Ridge as a place for a mid-ride rendezvous. After some initially sticky conversations, the Shack Riders agreed to move to a new site and eventually became advocates for Jasper Ridge's new-found reserve status and are among its generous financial supporters.

Once we had organized to protect the Ridge, a whole array of opportunities presented themselves. Paul S. Achilles, expressing a lifelong interest in the environment, made it possible to secure the Preserve and to undertake serious management of its resources—a task that Alan

Grundmann undertook and still performs. A faculty committee took charge of the scientific program, and long-term, protected research became possible.

Among the immediate beneficiaries were Paul Ehrlich's landmark studies of the ecology and evolution of the checkerspot butterfly, Hal Mooney's research on plant physiological ecology, and undergraduate courses on plant taxonomy and natural history that were taught for many years by renowned Ridge naturalist Herb Dengler.

When strong community interest developed in the botany, geology, and birdlife of the Ridge, a group of docents was organized and directed, first by Velinda Paranal and more recently by Monika Bjorkman. A course to train these docents has been a fixture in the Department of Biological Sciences for 15 years.

So what began as a modest conservation effort and as an attempt to protect continuing research has become a full-scale research facility and a community resource of inestimable importance. It gives vigorous life to field studies at Stanford; it is the terrestrial equivalent of the University's Hopkins Marine Station in Pacific Grove. It has encouraged a generation of research commitments by a remarkably distinguished assembly of population biologists. And now it is used by school children, by groups of citizens senior and not-so-senior, and by all those for whom the sight of goldfields in bloom in early April or a hillside greening after a January rain is balm for the soul.

I have to admit that my own need for Jasper Ridge these days falls into this last category. By dispensation from my colleagues in Biology, I still possess a key to the gate and pray annually for its retention. Especially when the pressures of institutional life grow heavy toward the end of April, I am apt to find myself driving through the gate, parking near the bridge at the upper end of the lake, and starting off on a walk.

The path leads through riverine woodland, whose trees are newly in leaf. I pause often and listen to hear whether the black-headed grosbeaks have returned on schedule. As the path turns around the end of the lake and rises into the chaparral, I look to the water for wood ducks and ring-necks, and on the ascent scan the manzanita to see if by chance this time the wrentits are violating their usual rule: that it is proper to be heard but not seen.

I listen for the first orange-crowned warbler in the oaks above, and I try to remember which path leads down to the rock where Monika showed me the Costanoan Indian acorn mill. My trip ends with a crossing of the dam, and a guess at how many weeks will pass before the streamflow in San Francisquito will be at summer levels.

The circuit never fails to produce a sense of peace and joy—and gratitude for our good fortune in being able to use this place in so many ways that benefit the human spirit.

DONALD KENNEDY

PRESIDENT

STANFORD UNIVERSITY

Stand of coastal redwoods near San Francisquito Creek

Natural light in an open-air laboratory

A Fragile Balance

Jasper Ridge means a great deal to me — indeed, it is one of the main things that has kept me at Stanford University for 31 years. It is difficult to overestimate the value of a 1,200-acre outdoor laboratory to a population biologist, especially such a facility right on campus. Indeed, to my knowledge, the Jasper Ridge Biological Preserve is the only such large laboratory located on the campus of a major research university. As such it has been an important element in keeping Stanford's Biology Department among the world's leaders.

The Preserve should be important to you, too. In a world of exploding human populations and rapidly disappearing natural habitat, it stands as a symbol of one university's determination to keep a sizable parcel of some of the most valuable non-urban land in the world from being developed. It suggests that even large, bureaucratic organizations can look up from the "bottom line" and vote to preserve non-monetary values.

And what a triumph it has been. I and my colleagues in biology benefitted enormously from the ease of doing field research in a wonderfully diverse local Preserve. And the things we have discovered at the Jasper Ridge Biological Preserve bear directly on the solutions of many of the problems that now threaten humanity—from feeding hungry people to keeping the atmosphere life-supporting rather than life-threatening. The millions of dollars of grant funds invested in the Preserve, and the many millions of dollars foregone in Stanford's decision not to develop it, have been returned to humanity many, many times over.

The Preserve has also provided Stanford with a great teaching facility. It serves as an outdoor classroom for courses in such areas as floristic botany, ornithology, and ecology. Many graduate students do their doctoral research on the Preserve, and many citizens of the Peninsula have been educated about natural history and the nature of field research through the excellent docent program.

There, of course, have been other great regional benefits. People of the Peninsula have a priceless piece of greenbelt; and those who admire wildflowers have a place to go in the spring where the spectacular floral display in serpentine grassland is protected. In the spring the nature tours pop up right along with the flowers. Birders can enjoy many interesting species, from spectacular wood ducks and osprey to elusive wrentits and fox sparrows.

Many's the time that, when marking and releasing butterflies, watching a coyote hunt, or enjoying "scoping" birds on the lake on a sparkling morning, I've reflected on a deep lesson to be learned from Jasper Ridge. It is that for a piece of land to be "valuable" it does not have to hold a subdivision, freeway, parking lot, factory, or shopping center. This is true globally, but it is especially true in an overpopulated, densely crowded, urban conglomeration such as the Bay Area has become. All of us can only hope that the lesson of Jasper Ridge will be heeded everywhere.

PAUL EHRLICH

BING PROFESSOR OF BIOLOGICAL SCIENCES

STANFORD UNIVERSITY

Female mallard with brood

A precious natural resource

A Journey Through Time

Many footsteps have passed through the island wilderness of Jasper Ridge, some quiet and careful of the land, others heavy with dreams and enterprise. Three thousand years ago, when the pyramids were rising over Egypt, Costanoan Indian families hunted in the Ridge's open grasslands, gathered acorns in the sun-soaked oak savanna, and fished in the Ridge's freshwater streams and pools. Later, in the 1760s, the Spanish began to arrive, bringing cattle and sheep and dreams of conquest. To sustain their growing numbers spiritually and physically, they cut down redwood stands to build missions and planted orchards, gardens, vineyards, and fields of grain.

In the 1800s, new Americans from Europe and migrants from the eastern states settled on the Ridge, logging blue oak, madrone, and redwood and excavating mines in unrealized hopes of finding veins of gold and silver ore. Then, after Stanford University was founded in 1885, researchers began to make their way up the Ridge by foot or horseback to study its rich variety of plants and animals. Through the 1960s, the public regularly traversed the Ridge to enjoy its lake and horseback trails.

In 1956, the University designated Jasper Ridge as academic reserve. Twenty years later, that protected status was granted more completely when the Board of Trustees formally designated 1200 acres as the Jasper Ridge Biological Preserve and closed the area to the public. Today, students and scholars from all over the world use the Preserve to study the subtle interactions of biological communities in a relatively undisturbed environment.

ANCIENT VILLAGE SITES

The first inhabitants of Jasper Ridge were ancestors of Costanoan or Ohlone Indians, hunting and gathering peoples who have traditionally inhabited the central coast of California between San Francisco and Point Sur. The names Ohlone and Costanoan are commonly used to refer to the Native American people who have inhabited the Bay Area for many thousands of years. *Oljón* was the name of one native village on the Pacific coast of San Mateo. Costanoan, another name used by Bay Area Native Americans, is derived from the Spanish term *costeño*, meaning "people of the coast."

Their presence on Jasper Ridge may date back 3200 years, as does a radiocarbon-dated village south of the Preserve on Adobe Creek. Stanford archaeologists have discovered eight prehistoric sites on the banks of San Francisquito Creek in what is now the Preserve, some of them villages and some of them smaller campsites. Others are areas where bedrock mortars were used for grinding acorns, grass seeds, and other foods. So far, only one of these villages has been radiocarbon dated; it was found to be approximately 1,000 years old. Together, the eight sites tell us about the history of the Ohlone or Costanoan Indians who made their home on Jasper Ridge.

Stanford studies show that Indian communities on what is now the Preserve were large, permanent villages like those found on the bay shore. Archaeologists can recognize village sites by their size, roughly equal to a city block, and by the dark gray or black color of the soil, which has been darkened by charcoal from fires and other organic debris. Bits of shell, stone tools, and other artifacts can still be seen in the earth, pushed up

This beautifully formed obsidian arrowhead, found in an archaeological excavation on the Jasper Ridge Biological Preserve, is called a "Stockton serrate." Such arrowheads are rarely found outside the

Sacramento Delta Region, where they were made 1,000 years ago. A symbolic arrow exchange with distant relatives or trading partners may have brought it to the people of Jasper Ridge.

from below by the activity of ground squirrels and pocket gophers.

Recent studies of mission records and other historic documents reveal that explorers found many such villages in the Peninsula's foothills. Records show that on December 7, 1774, Ohlones living near San Francisquito Creek invited Spanish explorers in the Rivera party to a feast in their honor at a village "near Portola Valley." The site of this feast may have been somewhere inside the Jasper Ridge Biological Preserve.

Mission records dating as early as 1769 indicate that several hundred people inhabited the San Francisquito area when Spanish explorers first arrived. About 80 archaeological sites have been found along San Francisquito Creek, so it seems probable that the entire watershed, including Jasper Ridge, was well populated long before the Spanish came to California. One village site on the Preserve, excavated by Stanford archaeologists from 1980 to 1982, is estimated to have had some 35 people living in it at any one time. Most Ohlone communities, called tribelets by anthro-

pologists, had several such villages. Constant visiting between all the villages along San Francisquito Creek would have kept the Jasper Ridge people in touch with neighbors and relatives.

In addition, these villagers were involved with larger trade and exchange networks from Monterey to Mono Lake. Evidence of trade found in village sites on the Preserve includes sea mussel, olivella, and abalone shells from the Pacific coast, 30 kilometers to the west, and San Francisco Bay, 10 kilometers to the east. Also found at sites on the Preserve are stone tools made of Monterey banded chert — probably from Point Año Nuevo, 40 kilometers to the southwest — and obsidian from the Napa and Sonoma valleys and from as far as Bodie Hills in the Sierra Nevada Mountains near Mono Lake.

SPANISH EXPLORERS

The first Europeans to visit Jasper Ridge arrived in 1769. They were members of a Spanish expedition led by Gaspar de Portolá and Franciscan missionary Juan Crespí. The Spanish viceroy in Mexico had directed Portolá to "rediscover" and explore the region of Monterey Bay. Portolá missed Monterey, however, and mistakenly headed inland toward the northeast. From the skyline of the San Francisco peninsula, the group sighted San Francisco Bay instead. On November 6, 1769, Portolá passed through the Jasper Ridge area on his way to the bay shore. The expedition followed San Francisquito Creek downstream and apparently camped near the tall redwood known as "El Palo Alto."

In 1774, another Spanish expedition passed through the hills west of Corte Madera Creek within view of Jasper Ridge. This was the Rivera party, accompanied by missionary Francisco Palou. Both Portolá and Rivera encountered many Indian villagers in the mid-Peninsula region and found them to be friendly and interested in Europeans. When Rivera's group feasted at Jasper Ridge in December 1774, both he and Palou were so taken with the native inhabitants and resources (specifically the redwoods) of the area that they recommended to the viceroy in Mexico that Mission San Francisco be founded on San Francisquito Creek. Instead, the Spanish chose to establish missions in San Francisco in 1776 and Santa Clara in 1777.

As soon as the first Spanish soldiers and missionaries arrived, logging, agriculture, and sheep and cattle grazing replaced the long-established Ohlone hunting and gathering tradition. The missions needed much land to support their populations, and San Francisquito Creek was identified as the boundary between Mission Santa Clara and Mission Dolores in San Francisco. Spanish settlers cultivated extensive grain fields in addition to gardens, orchards, and vineyards. They also immediately began cutting timber in the redwood forests along the creek to build the missions, and it is possible that trees were first removed from what is now the Preserve during this period. The forests by San Francisquito Creek must have been extensive; logging teams had to travel 15 to 25 miles from the mission communities to cut timbers there, and heavy loads had to be hauled back using ox-drawn wagons. Apparently, the supply was worth it. In 1841, a San José official noted that "San Francisquito redwoods" had been the Pueblo's best lumber source since San José was founded in 1777.

SETTLEMENT OF THE *CAÑADA*

After Mexico won independence from Spain in 1821, the Mexican government granted huge land tracts to its loyal new settlers in Alta California. The western half of the Jasper Ridge Biological Preserve lies within one such land grant, a 3,500-acre parcel known as *Rancho Cañada del Corte de Madera* (wood-cutting canyon). Máximo Martínez, a former soldier who was then alderman in San José, received this grant in 1834. Martínez was granted an additional 13,000 acres known as *Rancho Corte de Madera* in 1844. This much larger parcel included the remainder of what is now the Preserve.

While we have no records of logging activity from this early period, timber cutting may have increased in the late 1830s and 1840s as more and more settlers, first Mexican and then American, established homes and farms in the local area. We do know a little about grazing activities, however.

Martínez ran cattle, sheep, and horses on his Corte Madera lands, probably throughout the area's upper grassland and what is now the west lake shore inside the Jasper Ridge Biological Preserve.

THE AMERICANS ARRIVE

When California was declared a United States possession by American armed forces in 1846, settlers began to appear on the scene in increasing numbers. Compared to the eastern United States or to European countries, California seemed empty

Pedro Evancio, a Costanoan Indian of San Mateo County, photographed in the early 1890s

and unoccupied, and settlers were eager to acquire land for homes and farms. After Mexico formally ceded California to the United States in 1848, title to land became very uncertain, and the situation was further complicated by the swarms

Altar of the Church of St. Dennis

of settlers following the Gold Rush of 1849.

In the Jasper Ridge area, an Irish immigrant named Dennis Martin was one of the first Anglos to acquire land. After working for a year or so at Sutter's Fort near Sacramento, he traveled to the San Francisco Bay Area and ended up on Jasper Ridge, where he built a grist mill on San Francisquito Creek in 1846. He soon purchased a 1,200-acre parcel, where he planted orchards and built a home, barns, fences and corrals on lands now within the Preserve. In the 1850s, Martin constructed two sawmills on a hillside to the west of Jasper Ridge, and later he built a blacksmith shop, eight bunkhouses for mill workers, bridges, and a schoolhouse near his home. A few other private homes began to appear nearby, and when another school was built by the sawmill settlement, Martin converted his schoolhouse to a church. Another settler, John H. Sears, purchased some of Martin's western acreage. He built a house; later it was converted into a hotel he named Sears House. The mill town became the town of Searsville.

By the late 1860s, Searsville was a well-established and convenient stopover point between the logging camps of the foothills and the port of Redwood City. *McKenney's Pacific Coast Directory*, a listing published in San Francisco at that time, described the town as having a saloon called The Crystal Palace, a Wells Fargo office, a hotel, a store, a butcher shop, and a post office.

STRIKING SILVER

During the 1870s, mining interests added some short-lived local excitement to an economy otherwise based on grazing, farming, and logging. Searsville hotel proprietor August Eikerenkotter announced in May 1872 that silver had been discovered on his property to the south of Jasper Ridge. In August, a *Sacramento Daily Union* article reported a $20-per-ton gold mine not far from Searsville. Three years later, the Sacramento paper reported a silver lode on lands belonging to a Nicolas Larco in Searsville. Larco's mine allegedly produced ore at $150 to $250 per ton. In January 1876, another silver mine was reported on the western part of Jasper Ridge. Around this time, Larco's ranch foreman, Domenico Grosso, believed that he had discovered silver on eastern Jasper Ridge, and he persuaded Larco to purchase mineral rights from Dennis Martin.

None of the reports of silver mines were ever confirmed by later excavation. There were no more published accounts of new finds or of continued ore recovery from Jasper Ridge or Searsville lands. The privately published San Mateo County directory for 1875 lists 20 individuals in the Searsville area as farmers and only three persons as miners. In retrospect, nobody except real estate developers seems to have profited from the claims.

Awash in the romance of the past

Nevertheless, hope died hard for at least one man: Domenico Grosso. After Larco purchased the eastern Jasper Ridge mineral rights from Martin, Grosso supervised the excavation of two vertical mining shafts, one that was 75 feet deep and another that was nearly 200 feet deep. Larco went bankrupt in 1877 and turned over the

Jasper Ridge mineral rights to Grosso, who soon set up housekeeping on Jasper Ridge. He built a cabin, which he called The Palace Hotel, and he terraced the adjacent hillsides, where he planted olive and fruit trees and a vegetable garden.

Searsville Dam, completed in 1891

When University classes began in 1891, students began to explore the foothills and canyons of the Ridge. They became enamored of Grosso, nicknaming him "The Hermit," although by all accounts he was a friendly host to students and other occasional visitors. Until his death in 1915, Grosso believed that Jasper Ridge held valuable silver or gold ores, but he never found them. After his two original mine shafts filled with water in the early 1890s, he began to dig test pits throughout the surrounding area. Twenty such pits can still be found on the Preserve.

The town of Searsville itself disappeared during that period. In 1879, the United States District Court condemned Searsville's land for a new reservoir that would extend San Francisco's domestic water collection system. Most houses were moved away, and by the time the first classes were taught at Stanford University in 1891, Searsville Lake was filling with water for the first time.

A UNIVERSITY RESOURCE

From the University's first days, researchers relied on data from Jasper Ridge for their master's and doctoral theses. The first MS and PhD degrees based on Ridge research were awarded in 1896 and 1897. The master's thesis reviewed the genus manzanita (*Arctostaphylos*) and the first doctoral dissertation reported on reptiles of California and Oregon.

To accommodate scholars studying flora and fauna in the area, University zoologists built a cabin near San Francisquito Creek in 1900. Travel from campus took several hours each way, by foot or horseback, and the cabin was a convenient overnight stopping place. Between 1900 and 1920, a total of 20 advanced degrees were granted to students working on or near Jasper Ridge. Their subjects ranged from winter-blooming plants to trapdoor spiders and tarantulas to the chemical constituents of water in San Francisquito Creek.

Research efforts intensified in the 1920s. Nineteen more advanced degrees were granted between 1921 and 1930, again on a wide range of topics—from limnology (the scientific study of the chemical and biological properties of lakes and ponds) to the ever-popular venomous spiders. In 1923, A.G. Vestal began a long-term study of the effects of cattle grazing on local vegetation. Also in the early 1920s, a group of geology and mining students returned to re-excavate Grosso's original mine shaft, which was no small task. Timbers lining the top of the shaft had caved in, creating an

immense logjam 20 feet underground. More-over, the entire 187-foot shaft had filled with water; even after clearing, it refilled with 17 feet of water every 24 hours. Despite such obstacles, the students began operations in the mine and

The bustle of Searsville Resort in the 30s

uncovered a narrow vein of ore with minute traces of gold, silver, lead, zinc, and copper. Unfortunately, the ore had no economic value. In 1923, the Mining Department announced that they planned to continue to use the shafts and test pits to give students practical experience in mining techniques.

A LOCAL RESORT

While biologists and geologists were increasingly drawn to the research possibilities of the Jasper Ridge area, the public was increasingly interested in its recreational possibilities. The University purchased the dam, lake, and northwest Jasper Ridge parcel from the Spring Valley Water Company in 1916. Then, in 1922, Stanford swim coach Ernie Bransten leased rights to the lake and its eastern hillside from the University and opened Searsville Lake Park. Bransten constructed a parking area, dressing rooms, and an entrance bridge over San Francisquito Creek. In 1927, the park was expanded to include the lake's west shore. With a larger area to operate, Bransten developed Searsville Lake into a local resort. He imported sand from Santa Cruz County for a beach and built a snack bar and caretaker's house. He even added a three-tiered diving tower to the top of the dam.

In 1922, when the park was first opened, the Woodside Trail Club was formed and gained access to Jasper Ridge for horseback riding. A decade later, the Menlo Circus Club built a shed to provision cross-country riders near the site of the Hillside Lab. In the late 1940s an informal group known as Rooney's Rough Riders adopted the shed, christening it "The Shack." The group eventually incorporated as The Shack Riders, Inc. and rebuilt the shed, adding picnic tables and hitching racks.

Academic and recreational use continued together at Jasper Ridge from the 1920s through the 1960s. During these four decades, another 52 advanced degrees were awarded to biology, geology, and engineering students who used the Jasper Ridge area as a natural laboratory. By the early 1950s, however, the postwar housing boom was expanding the local population. Swimmers and boaters flocked to Searsville Lake, and riders visited the trails in ever-increasing numbers.

COMMITMENT TO STEWARDSHIP

In 1956, the Stanford Board of Trustees moved to protect Jasper Ridge from development by designating the Ridge, including the lake and swamp areas, as academic reserve. This newly awarded status demonstrated the University's strong commitment to supporting continued research in the reserve. In 1959, Paul Ehrlich began his many-decade study of the Bay checkerspot butterfly (*Euphydryas editha*) population in the reserve's serpentine grassland. And during this time, Jasper Ridge was first described in a publication as Stanford's "biological experimental area."

Cattle grazing was no longer permitted in the upper grasslands by 1960, and public use was increasingly restricted by signs and trail closures. During the 1960s, the University also argued successfully against a proposed Army Corps Dam across San Francisquito Creek that would have inundated much of the wilderness experimental area. The dam was never built.

In the 1970s the University took more formal steps to protect Jasper Ridge. The Department of Biological Sciences arranged for the Westridge fence to be built, defining the 1.5-mile southern border of the Ridge. In 1973, the Board of Trustees designated a 960-acre parcel, including the Ridge, grasslands, swamp, and inner marsh, as

the Jasper Ridge Biological Preserve and hired a part-time administrative director to manage the Preserve lands. The University also renegotiated the Searsville Park lease, and the resort opened for its 1973 season under much more restricted terms, with public access limited to the west lakeshore. However, there were increasing problems with vandalism and disruption to the Preserve as well as to neighboring communities.

Water roars over the keystone dam

The University bought out the Searsville Park lease in 1976 and closed the area to the general public. The Board of Trustees formally expanded the Preserve to 1,200 acres, adding the lake and lands to its west, outer marsh areas, and the narrow strip of land between San Francisquito Creek and the Stanford Linear Accelerator. The last proved to be an especially valuable addition, since five of the Preserve's eight archaeological sites were discovered in this area, on the northern bank of the creek.

In recent years, the Jasper Ridge Biological Preserve has drawn scholars from 30 universities in seven countries to conduct research in one of the very few natural biological preserves located so near to a major university. A total of 139 advanced degrees have been awarded based on Jasper Ridge research, and undergraduates as well as graduate students visit the Preserve almost daily to study its biological, geological, and archaeological resources. Not just academics but local naturalists as well value the Preserve as an island of near-wild nature in an increasingly urban environment: a living laboratory in which to observe natural environmental systems.

Old oak holding silent vigil over Stanford and the bay view

RODENT DISTURBANCE

The work of Stanford archaeologists excavating Ohlone sites at the Jasper Ridge Biological Preserve has been both helped and hindered by the competing excavations of ground squirrels, pocket gophers, and other burrowing rodents that inhabit the Preserve. These species move through the earth almost as easily as we move through air. As they tunnel underground, they eat edible roots and displace everything else in their paths, including rocks, worms, and archaeological artifacts. To clear the tunnel of accumulated loose soil, they burrow straight up toward the surface, open a small hole, and dump out the soil and all it contains. In one year, pocket gophers burrowing under a Quad-size meadow could displace 23 metric tons of earth. From an archaeologist's perspective, they make identifying sites an easier job by depositing artifacts on the surface. But they also cause considerable confusion by moving them from the places where they were originally abandoned.

As a gopher tunnels, it gathers up artifacts smaller than the 6-centimeter diameter of its burrow and dumps them on the surface. Correspondingly, Stanford archaeologists have found most small pieces of bone, shell, and stone concentrated in a "rodent zone" within 20 centimeters of the surface. Experimental work has shown that every 17 years, the artifacts in this rodent zone are completely replaced by others as a result of burrowing activity.

When a gopher encounters objects larger than 6 centimeters, however, it cannot dislodge

Gophers upset archaeological chronology

them and instead burrows beneath these obstacles. This activity slowly undermines large objects and causes them to settle into a layer about 40 centimeters below the surface. Archaeologists studying sites on the Preserve have found most large artifacts at those deeper levels.

Without understanding the effects of rodent disturbance, Stanford archaeologists would still be trying to explain why the biggest artifacts, the heaviest chunks of animal bone, and the largest shell species predominate in the deeper levels of the sites. Since in an undisturbed site, the deepest layers are the oldest, researchers might have hypothesized that early inhabitants collected different species of shellfish and made different types of tools. They might have also concluded that, for some unknown reason, a layer of fist-sized rocks was deliberately scattered across the entire village. A more probable explanation is rodent disturbance — the manic activity level of pocket gophers and their inability to move objects larger than their heads.

Bedrock mortars used by Costanoans to grind acorns

ARCHAEOLOGY RESEARCH

Since the early 1970s, Stanford faculty, staff, and students have been investigating the eight Ohlone sites that have been found on the Jasper Ridge Biological Preserve. The best known of the smaller sites is Rattlesnake Rock, a steep hillside on the northwest corner of the Preserve. Student archaeologists have found 37 bedrock mortars (bowl-shaped holes of various sizes pecked into rock) among the site's tumbled boulders and bedrock exposures. Common throughout California, bedrock mortars are believed to have been used for grinding acorns, grass seeds, and other foods. Several large mortars on the Preserve, however, are found near the very top of the steep rock face on inaccessible, narrow ledges. These may have been used for other purposes — rainmaking, perhaps. Some California Indian groups refer to these as "rain rocks" and describe ceremonies that use them to summon rain clouds.

In 1980, Stanford archaeologists began excavating one large village site comprising 4,800 square meters, about one third the size of Stanford's Inner Quad. From 1980 to 1982, the team of archaeologists and 75 Stanford students and volunteers excavated a 1% sample of the village and unearthed 500 stone and bone tools; 160 shell beads, pendants, and other ornaments; 2,500 metric tons of fire-cracked rock from hearths and earth ovens; 2,200 pieces of animal bone from 35 different mammals, fish, and birds; and 150,000 shell fragments from 30 types of San Francisco Bay and Pacific Ocean shellfish. In the center of the village were found two clusters of burned rock, shell, and animal bone fragments, the remains, perhaps, of two groups of houses and hearths. Based on the size of the village and the distribution of household artifacts within it, Stanford archaeologists estimate that some 35 people lived there at any one time. Studies of this village and other Ohlone sites on the Preserve continue today as part of the University's Campus Archaeology Program.

Dennis Martin, an Irish immigrant who settled on Jasper Ridge in the 1840s, went from boom to bust in the turbulent years following the Gold Rush. One of the first Anglos to purchase land in the Jasper Ridge area, Martin built a grist mill in 1846, followed by a home, a barn, a blacksmith shop, a schoolhouse, and two sawmills and bunkhouses for the millworkers. In 1856, the Archbishop of San Francisco visited Jasper Ridge to celebrate Mass and to dedicate the schoolhouse that Martin converted to the Church of St. Dennis; it was the area's first church.

Martin's larger mill operated with 26 saws, two edgers, and a planer. The *San Mateo County Gazette* reported in 1859 that his two mills together could produce 24,000 board-feet of lumber per day. It is almost certain that, during this period, Martin or one of his competitors cut timber within what today is the Preserve. Martin or others also began clearing the Preserve's blue oak woodland; the many stump-sprouted trees in the woodland of today are evidence of their work. Many trees were also cut by charcoal burners in the 1850s and 1860s. While there are no records of such activity on Jasper Ridge, documents show that dozens of large oak and madrone trees from Rancho San Francisquito (now part of the Stanford University campus) were converted into charcoal and were shipped to San Francisco.

The late 1850s marked a rapid decline in Martin's fortunes. He lost the smaller of his mills to creditors, and he was forced to sell the larger mill to pay property taxes. The new owners moved the mill to La Honda, where it burned down in 1859. Martin continued to have difficulties paying his taxes, and a legal battle began for title to his 1200-acre parcel in what is now the Preserve. His home, church, and orchard were in jeopardy, as was the rest of his property on the north side of San Francisquito Creek.

In 1864 Martin finally lost title to much of his land, and he and his family were forced to abandon their home, church, and orchards. Luckily, Martin had purchased 900 acres on the south side of the creek in 1856; this parcel encompassed the eastern two thirds of the present-day Preserve and part of the adjoining Webb Ranch. Martin moved his family across the creek, and his activities continued on Jasper Ridge lands. In the 1870s he sold his mineral rights on the Ridge to a local rancher, Nicolas Larco. Larco eventually sold the mineral rights to his ranch foreman, Domenico

Grosso, and Grosso went on to become a famous would-be miner and eccentric known to a generation of early University students.

In 1881, Martin's last local holdings were sold by the sheriff for taxes, although Martin continued his court battles to recover his lands north of the creek for several more years. Martin died in San Francisco in 1890, leaving several daughters and their families in the vicinity of Jasper Ridge.

Church of St. Dennis, consecrated in 1856

Serpentine, oak woodland, and chaparral

BIRTH IN UPHEAVAL

West of the Jasper Ridge Biological Preserve, in the steep and woody coastal hills, a brooding shadow carves a path below the skyline and snakes north beyond the line of sight. It is the San Andreas fault, winding past the Preserve and valley to the east while it pauses in its earth-convulsing work.

While the San Andreas has been rightfully feared for its violence in historic times, it is but one of hundreds of named and unnamed faults that slice across the continent's western edge. And its force is just a whisper of the seismic fury that created the Ridge and its environs more than 100 million years ago.

The distorted geology of the Preserve is vivid evidence that its birth — like that of much of the Northern California coast — was in all likelihood not a gentle process. The Ridge as it exists today is the result of vast and violent changes occurring over titanic periods of time. Most of these changes are the result of plate movement and erosion. It is now well accepted that the earth's crust is divided into huge plates that move about over deeper molten material. At the boundaries where two plates meet, material from within the earth can upwell; this can cause the plates to spread further apart, or one plate can override another, or the plates can slip past each other. The San Andreas fault, which crosses the western edge of the Preserve, is the boundary between the North American and Pacific plates, which are slipping past each other at a rate of about 5 centimeters per year.

A S I N K I N G P L A T E

The birth of Jasper Ridge, however, resulted from the overriding of one ancient crustal plate by

Scarsville Lake, the dam and the developing delta

another. Some 100 to 150 million years ago, when dinosaurs dominated the land, the Farallon plate, a now long-vanished oceanic segment of the earth's crust, was sliding inexorably underneath the North American continent. As it sank, ocean sediment, lava from undersea eruptions, and other geological debris were scraped off onto the surface of North America's western edge. These ancient ocean-bottom residues make up the Franciscan geologic formation, the material that forms most of the Ridge.

Later, perhaps 50 million years ago, when mammals began to scramble up the evolutionary ladder, rivers carried inland mud and sand down to the sea and deposited them near the coast. This gritty material was gradually cemented together to form Eocene sandstone, which over time rose up on the land in mountainous formations. Today, these Eocene sandstone slopes, carved and catacombed by time, are strikingly visible on the northern and eastern sides of the Preserve.

We know little of what the land that is now the Preserve looked like in the first few million years after the Farallon plate disappeared beneath the continent. It may have been the bottom of a stream valley. We do know, however, that about 2 to 3 million years ago, the California Coast Ranges, including the Santa Cruz Mountains, began to thrust up from the earth's crust, bowing the Franciscan formation rock into an arch. The softer rocks above the Franciscan formation then eroded away, and the steep-sided, flat-topped hill we now know as Jasper Ridge emerged. As the coastal mountains uplifted, alluvial material accumulated in a basin to the west and north of Jasper Ridge and formed the youngest rocks of the Preserve, the Santa Clara geological formation.

The legacy of this tumultuous geologic history is an extraordinary collection of very different rocks within the Preserve's small area. Over time, these rocks have been broken down by wind, water, and acids from plant roots into a richly diverse mix of soils. Each type of soil supports a different variety of plants, which in turn supports a different segment of the animal populations on

the Preserve. This unusual diversity of rocks, soils, plants, and animals, so close to a major university, makes possible such varied research.

FROM EARTH'S MANTLE

Much of the rock on Jasper Ridge was formed

Serpentine's Springtime palette

on the bottom of the sea: greenstone, derived from lava erupted deep under the ocean surface, and the reddish chert, composed of the remnants of single-celled marine organisms. But in many ways the most interesting rock on the Jasper Ridge Biological Preserve is serpentine, which has even deeper origins. A greenish-gray rock, serpentine

Goldfields, California poppies, and linanthus

originated far below the earth's surface in the upper mantle, the layer beneath the crust. It was squeezed up in a narrow, discontinuous band, at most 100 meters across, where the Franciscan formation contacts the North American plate at what must have been a major fault line.

Chemically, serpentine contains abundant magnesium and very little calcium, a pattern opposite to that of most rocks. Serpentine also contains unusually large amounts of nickel and aluminum. As a result of this peculiar composition, serpentine gives rise to a soil that is toxic to many plants, including some of the introduced grasses that dominate California's grasslands. The native plants that are able to thrive on serpentine soils, therefore, are protected from competition with introduced grasses that dominate on other parts of the Preserve. It is these native plants that, in springtime, create the beautiful floral displays for which Jasper Ridge is famous.

GREENSTONE: RED ROCK

Greenstone, derived from oceanic lava, is the most abundant type of rock at the Preserve. It is so named because it appears greenish when fresh, but because it is high in iron, it turns red when exposed to oxygen, even when deep in the soil. Generations of students have been taught to recognize greenstone by its red color.

As greenstone breaks down, it gives rise to a more "typical" soil than does serpentine, richer in nutrients and able to support a wider variety of plants. Because of this comparative richness, it is

Hospitality in sandstone

more easily dominated by introduced species than the serpentine-derived soil. As a result, the contrast between the green wild oats that dominate on greenstone soils and the brilliant yellows and oranges of the flowers that dominate on serpentine soils is a pleasing sight during a spring hike.

RIDGE OF JASPER

Chert, derived from microscopic marine organisms, is the rock that gives the Preserve its name, because chert stained by iron oxides is called jasper. A very hard, silica-rich rock that will scratch steel, chert is the "flint" that Native Americans used for arrowheads. It is much less abundant than greenstone and breaks down very slowly under the influence of air, water, and acids. As a result, the patches of chert at the Preserve tend to be on hilltops. They have shallow soils and support relatively slow plant growth.

SCULPTED SANDSTONE

A highlight of any walk through the Preserve are the dramatic Eocene sandstone formations on its northern and eastern sides. Gaping caves and hollows formed by centuries of rain flow and erosion have sculpted the smooth-sided sandstone cliffs. The cement that binds together the individual grains of sand breaks down relatively easily under the influence of water, giving rise to a deep, sandy soil. The plants and animals on soil derived from sandstone are like those on greenstone soils.

A ramble across the Jasper Ridge Biological Preserve is a ramble across 150 million years of often-violent history. That violence continues today. The San Andreas fault ruptured in 1906, displacing fences in Portola Valley between 7 and 9 feet. The Loma Prieta section of the fault convulsed in 1989, and the chances are approximately one in four that the San Andreas will awake again before the year 2020, as the Pacific plate moves slowly northward past the North American Plate.

F I E L D   N O T E
HERMIT MINE

In 1872, August Eikerenkotter, a hotelier in Searsville, declared that he had discovered silver on his property, and locals became excited about the prospect of finding silver ore on Jasper Ridge. Twenty years later, however, mine shafts and numerous test pits had yielded nothing of value except perhaps a store of local legend — most of those stories concerned Domenico Grosso.

Grosso, an Italian miner who owned mineral rights on Jasper Ridge, lived meagerly in one of the Ridge's western canyons until his death in 1915. He was known affectionately as "The Hermit" to hundreds of Stanford students who picnicked and hiked in the area.

The absence of valuable ores on the Ridge was later confirmed in the early 1920s, when Stanford geology and mining students re-excavated one of the shafts and found only minute traces of gold, silver, zinc, lead, copper and other minerals.

Domenico Grosso, "The Hermit"

Serpentine grassland
before the burst of
spring

Soft sandstone worn by centuries of erosion

Rattlesnake Rock, reminder of the Costanoan past

Spring yields to summer and grasses turn gold

GRASSLANDS
SEEDS OF CHANGE

The golden hills of summer are, for many, the image of the "real" California. From May until November, the grassy, straw-colored hills roll like endless waves across the state, here and there broken by live oaks or an outcropping of rock. At the Jasper Ridge Biological Preserve, the grasslands, rich and green in spring, are dried to a flaxen color by summer drought. Walking through a tall field of grass in July, it's easy to daydream of Spaniards and adventurers and the unspoiled, rustic life of "old California."

What irony it is, then, to discover that the "typical" California grasses are not native to this state at all, but were carried here inadvertently from Spain as hay on cattle ships bound for the New World. Other alien seeds made their way overland on cattle drives from Spanish Mexico. Over time, these invading grasses, whose seeds dispersed efficiently by attaching to fur and clothing, completely dominated the over-grazed native grasslands, transforming the face and color of California.

HISTORY IN MISSION BRICKS

A unique record of the arrival of these alien species is contained in the adobe bricks of the Spanish missions. The bricks that were formed earliest contain seeds of only a few invaders, while the bricks of later missions have a much larger representation of the seeds of Old World species.

Mostly annuals, the dominant alien grasses are wild oats *(Avena* spp.*)*, wild rye *(Lolium*

Goldfields, tidy tips, and linanthus

multiflorum), and species of brome *(Bromus* spp.*)* and annual non-grass herbaceous plants (called forbs) such as filaree *(Erodium* spp.*)*. These invasive species germinate with the first rains of fall and die when the drought begins in late spring. All summer long their dried and golden stalks stand, covering the hills. In the fall the rains come

and the grasses decompose, releasing minerals that nourish the newly germinating plants. Then the cycle starts again.

What were the pristine California grasslands like before they were supplanted by the Old World grasses? Unfortunately, we do not have any precise written descriptions. Some clues, however, can be found at the Preserve. Here, and in other places in Northern California, are isolated grasslands of a totally different nature, found on soils derived from serpentine rock. These soils lack adequate amounts of nutrients, such as nitrogen and phosphorous, that most plants require. Moreover, they contain high concentrations of toxic metals, such as nickel.

Most plants grow very poorly on these soils, yet there is abundant plant life on these islands of serpentine. And the plants found on serpentine are almost entirely native species. Annual forbs predominate, but there is good representation of perennial grasses and forbs. Many of these serpentine forbs have brightly colored flowers, creating in early spring a brilliant mosaic of annual and perennial forbs against a green backdrop of perennial bunch grasses.

Goldfields *(Lasthenia)* cover the serpentine in spring. Yellow and white tidy tips *(Layia)*, pink linanthus *(Linanthus)*, and golden California poppies *(Eschscholzia)* are also present in abundance. Their brightly colored flowers attract many flying insect pollinators, another characteristic that sets the serpentine community apart from the mainly wind-pollinated non-serpentine grasses.

Some scientists believe that all of California's native grasslands were once similar to these serpentine communities. Instead of endless hills of green or gold, California before the Spanish may have been a blazing patchwork of yellows, pinks, and oranges from the mountains to the sea.

Two Grassland Worlds

How have the serpentine grasslands protected themselves against invading species? It seems that the introduced grasses are unable to tolerate the poor growing conditions of serpentine soils. In fact, by simply applying fertilizer to serpentine soil, one can totally alter the character

of the grassland, allowing invading grasses to replace most of the native forbs and grasses.

Hiking on the crest of the Ridge, one discovers well-developed grasslands dominated by either native or introduced species. That is because

Brilliant carpet half a mile long

the ridge top is the contact between two soils, one derived from serpentine and the other from greenstone. In springtime, you do not need a geological map to tell you which soil type you are standing on; the serpentine community is a palette of color, while the rest of the grassland is the uniform green of the introduced grasses. The contrast between these grasslands can be seen clearly from an airplane.

The juxtaposition of these two grassland worlds on the Jasper Ridge Biological Preserve also provides unique glimpses of the interaction of plants and animals in grassland ecosystems. During a year, one square meter of introduced grassland produces about four times more plant material than does an equal area of serpentine grassland, providing more protective cover for small birds and animals. The meadowlark nests in the tall, dense invading grasses, but feeds in the serpentine community, where it finds abundant food in the open vegetation. Mice and voles,

too, generally keep to the more protective cover of non-serpentine grassland. Gophers, on the other hand, prefer the serpentine community because a major food source abounds there, and, because they live underground, they do not need continuous overhead vegetation to protect them from predatory birds.

On the Preserve, most springtime travelers are drawn to the serpentine grasslands for their startling beauty. But for scientists and others who peer beneath their flowering surface, the rare islands of serpentine contain hidden worlds of plant and animal relationships that reflect a California long past.

Mariposa lily among wild oats

Western meadowlark among tarweed

California
poppies in
a bed of
linanthus

FIELD NOTE
BAY CHECKERSPOT BUTTERFLY

Like plant communities, animal populations often display special adaptations to changes or variations in the climate. Since 1960, population biologist Paul Ehrlich and his research group have been conducting a classic, long-term study of the population of Jasper Ridge's checkerspot butterflies *(Euphydryas editha)*, insects that gather nectar from serpentine flowers such as tidy tips, hog fennel, and linanthus (*Linanthus*). Ehrlich has tracked the interactions of this small species and the Preserve's climate and microclimates in great detail.

Ehrlich found that the butterflies' caterpillars are in a race to grow before summer drought sets in. The females lay their eggs on or near tiny annual plantains (*Plantago erecta*), relatives of common garden weeds. In April, hatching caterpillars, or larvae, feed communally on the plantains and immediately find themselves in a struggle for survival: they must grow large enough to endure California's summer drought before their food plants dry up, or they will perish.

Most of them don't make it. The ones that survive do so because they are lucky. Perhaps the plantain that the larvae are feeding on is in a favorable spot such as a moist hollow. If so, it may last long enough for the larvae to grow large enough to enter the resting stage in which they must pass the summer. Or, more likely, the larvae have managed to leave their drying plantain and find a plant of owl's clover (*Orthocarpus densiflorus*), which they are also able to eat and which dries later.

When the winter rains come, the caterpillars are aroused from their enforced summer rest and begin feeding again. When they start, they are less than half an inch long, and they must multiply their weight many times before they can form chrysalids (pupae), the stage at which the caterpillar metamorphoses into an adult butterfly. The speed with which they can grow depends on patterns of rainfall and sunlight and the topography of their habitat. Weather patterns and slope combine to create "microclimates" which determine the pace of the butterflies' development. A caterpillar in a favorable microclimate may be ready to form the pupa two weeks before one in an unfavorable microclimate. The

offspring of both will be once again in a race with the drying of the food plant. As a result, the microclimate exerts very strong evolutionary pressure on the species.

Understanding the ways in which environmental factors control the size of the checkerspot populations on the Jasper Ridge Biological Preserve has provided insight into problems as diverse as how to control populations of insects that attack crops (insects are humanity's most important competitor for food) and how to design nature reserves to protect beneficial insects.

Black-tailed deer camouflaged by the dusky summer landscape

Native bunch grasses dot the Ridge

FIELD NOTE
GOPHERS

Many gardeners view gophers as pests that gobble up roots, bulbs, and occasionally entire plants. On the Preserve, too, the gopher is voracious; in the process of its energetic digging, it plays a central role in determining the variety and location of plants in the serpentine grassland.

The gopher commonly found in the Preserve is Botta's pocket gopher, or *Thomomys bottae*. These large-toothed rodents burrow below ground and deposit mounds of loose subsoil on the surface. Research indicates that during the span of one year, roughly one quarter of the surface area of the Preserve's serpentine grassland may be covered by new mounds. This disturbance affects the makeup of the serpentine community.

Because gopher mounds consist of subsoil, not overturned topsoil, they have lower concentrations of organic matter and nutrients and higher concentrations of some minerals that are toxic to plants. As a result, plants grown under controlled conditions in gopher mound soil produce less biomass than plants grown in undisturbed serpentine soil. Some species are more sensitive than others to the chemical differences between undisturbed serpentine soils and gopher mounds. One would expect these sensitive species to be less abundant in areas chronically disturbed by these rodents.

To test this hypothesis, researchers excluded gophers from several areas of the serpentine for five years. In those areas, the researchers detected increases in *Brodiaea* species, the yellow-flowered goldfields (*Lasthenia*), and two species of perennial bunch grasses. It therefore appears likely that the composition of the serpentine depends significantly on the presence of gophers.

Brown towhee

The chemical makeup of serpentine and greenstone explain the presence of vastly different vegetation growing on the adjoining soils. In spring, the serpentine is ablaze with colorful native wildflowers. On greenstone, the monchromatic alien grasses provide protective cover for birds and other animals.

Black-tailed deer reclining in the cool of the day

Spring wild flowers

A major influence on plants of Jasper Ridge serpentine grasslands is the harvester ant (*Veromessor andrei*). In a hectare of grassland, there may be more than 100 ant nests below ground, each housing legions of ants. Beginning in early spring, these ants selectively harvest the fruits or seeds of a number of serpentine annuals. One of the first annuals to flower is shining pepper grass (*Lepidium nitidum*). The ants use their mouth parts to cut or break off *Lepidium* fruits while the drying plants are still standing. Fruits or seeds of many other species are collected after the seeds have dispersed. The ants bring the fruits back to their nests and discard unused parts around the nest entrance.

Stanford faculty and students have documented several ways the ants affect the distribution of serpentine plants. The ants remove a large proportion of the fruits of preferred species, such as the dandelion relative *Microseris douglasii*, and consequently this species is less abundant in areas where ant nests are most numerous. Research has also shown that some plant species occur most often — and sometimes almost exclusively — on the middens encircling the nest entrances. For some species such as the brightly colored red maids (*Calandrinia ciliata*), this probably results when harvested seeds are left or discarded outside the nest, but the presence of some other species remains a mystery. A possible factor is that the debris discarded by the ants adds nutrients, particularly phosphorus, to the soil around their nests, and this may favor some species over others.

Building Storm

Narrow-leaved mule ears, member of the sunflower family

Hillside shot with gold

F I E L D   N O T E
G R A S S L A N D S   I N V A S I O N

What happens to plant populations as a result of Northern California's dramatic variation in annual rainfall? The changing borders between grassland and chaparral may provide some answers to this question.

Aerial photographs of Jasper Ridge dating back to the 1930s provide a record of the invasion of coyote brush (*Baccharis pilularis* var *consanguinea*) in a draw (a gently sloping valley) at the southeast end of the grassland. Here the coyote brush first appeared in the 1940s. Its expansion was very slow, and coyote brush grew only in the wettest part of the draw until the late 1970s. At that time, the number of plants and the area they occupied began to increase dramatically; they were filling in the draw. The largest number of plants appeared during 1982-83, a year of exceptionally high rainfall. This dense stand of coyote brush now consists of mature shrubs that can withstand even severe drought years and provides sufficient cover to enable other woody plants to establish themselves.

The amount of annual rainfall also determines the abundance of soft chess (*Bromus mollis*), a grass native to Eurasia but present in the serpentine grassland. In dry years, this species is mostly confined to non-serpentine soils, but in years of high rainfall it invades the serpentine community. This pattern, detected through long-term studies of climate and vegetation, suggests that heavy rainfall favors invading species over native species in the serpentine grassland.

Long-term studies like these are necessary for detecting gradual changes in vegetation, and may enable scientists to predict changes resulting from human activities.

Turret spider nest on yerba buena

Scarlet pimpernel

Black-tailed deer

F I E L D   N O T E
The Bare Zone

Within the Preserve's grasslands are scattered islands of dry and shrubby chaparral. Where the grassland and chaparral meet, there is almost always a barren swath of about a meter or so in width. This has been called the "bare zone."

For many years, ecologists had attributed this naked border to the herbicidal or inhibiting effects of aromatic compounds released by the shrubs.

But a Stanford study conducted in 1970 by Bruce Bartholomew, now at the California Academy of Sciences, found another explanation.

Bartholomew placed C-shaped hardware-cloth fences (called exclosures) in the bare zone with the opening facing the grassland. He observed that as long as these animal exclosures protected the bare zone from forays by chaparral-dwelling

herbivores, plants grew abundantly in this so-called "toxic" zone. He concluded that the small rodents, rabbits, and birds that cling to the chaparral for cover forage intensively in the neighboring grassland. From records of their activity, such as the location of rabbit pellets, he found that these animals venture no farther than necessary into the grassland, where their protection from predators is minimal. Thus, on the Preserve, animal activity accounts for the bare zone where chaparral and grassland meet. Now featured in textbooks in introductory biology, this study was an important demonstration of the role of vertebrates in controlling vegetation patterns.

The vegetation itself plays a role in maintaining vegetation boundaries by limiting the ability of shrubs to take hold in the grassland. Shrub seeds that germinate in grassland must out-compete resident grasses for moisture near the soil surface, then send a tap root deep enough to find

moisture during their first summer drought, and finally, escape browsing by deer or other animals. This year-long triathlon claims virtually all shrub seeds that germinate in grassland.

Ground squirrel on a housekeeping mission

Stately valley oak is home to numerous species of birds

All of the many species of fungi on the Preserve are important agents of decomposition. They have a variety of ecologic relationships with other organisms; many are symbiotic or parasitic.

Fungi artistry

Mariposa lily

This white mariposa lily is one of several species of *Calochortus* on the Preserve. The lily originates from a bulb and waits to flower until the end of spring, when the surrounding grasses have dried.

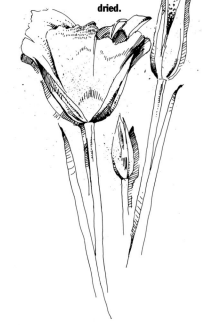

In summer, the grasses scatter their seeds

Califorina sage borders the chaparral

CHAPARRAL
LIFE BY FIRE

L ike cataclysmic clockwork, the gentle California landscape is regularly wracked by earthquakes and ravaged by fire, especially in the kindling-dry chaparral of the coastal mountains and Sierra Nevada foothills. Dominated by tough and hard-leaved shrubs, chaparral is a community designed to burn. And burn it does, on average every 20 years in the drier parts of the state, with an awesome fury and destructive power.

The most common chaparral shrub is the highly flammable chamise (*Adenostoma fasciculatum)*, characterized by fine branches and leaves rich in incendiary compounds. Other chaparral shrubs such as scrub oak (*Quercus durata*), toyon (*Heteromeles arbutifolia*), manzanita (*Arctostaphylos* spp.), and red berry (*Rhamnus crocea*) are also highly combustible. With the proper climatic conditions — hot and dry weather, desiccating winds, or rare summer lightning storms — these shrubs can ignite, causing intensive and devastating conflagrations.

Climbing up the south- and southwest-facing slopes of Jasper Ridge, and on top of the Preserve as well, one finds well-developed chaparral that, out of deference to the Preserve's neighbors, has been protected from the ravages of fire. This area was, in fact, the site of one of the first detailed studies ever made of the California chaparral community. A pioneering ecologist, William S. Cooper, visited Stanford University in the late 1920s and established a number of long-term observation plots in the area to study the relationship between plant and leaf structure and the dry California summer climate. A few of his plots are still recognizable today, giving a clear demonstration of the slow rate of change in this community when fire is prevented. Cooper, and researchers who followed him, have described special features of chaparral shrubs that enable them to endure severe summer drought.

ADAPTED TO DROUGHT

Shrubs of the chaparral hold their small, hard leaves throughout the year, and some species retain their leaves for several years. During the summer drought, the hard leaves are better able to withstand water stress than are the thin leaves of many other plants. The small size of the leaves is another advantage. In the bright sun of summer, large leaves become excessively warm. The small-leaved chaparral shrubs, however, are able to avoid damage from high temperatures. By withstanding drought instead of losing their leaves during the season, the chaparral shrubs can capture energy from the sun during dry periods and store it for use during favorable growing periods.

Vulnerability to insects and grazing animals is the price they pay for having leaves throughout the year. In self-defense, the leaves of chaparral plants contain an immense array of toxic compounds. The leaves are further defended by their toughness, which makes them disagreeable to chewing insects and other grazing animals.

RENEWED BY FLAMES

When the water-starved chaparral shrubs are ignited, they burn with intense destructive power. But the chaparral blaze does not destroy all life in its path. A mature chaparral stand supports large numbers of plants and animals, and when fire comes, even an intense one, many will survive. Birds—owls, California quail, thrashers, wrentits, and brown towhees—take wing. Mobile animals find shelter in the concealing

The dense canopy of the chaparral is nearly impenetrable to humans, but the buck brush, manzanita, and chamise provide good grazing for black-tailed deer. Chamise, the most common chaparral shrub, is also known as greasewood because it is so flammable.

manzanita

thickets; brush rabbits, dusky-footed woodrats, gophers, mice, skunks, and reptiles can move ahead of the flames or escape into existing burrows to insulate themselves from the intense surface heat. A chaparral burn rejuvenates the landscape. A year after the blaze, an almost magical transformation takes place. Instead of appearing as scorched earth or woody shrubs, the chaparral community becomes a carpet of flowering herbaceous plants, brilliant with western poppies (*Papaver californicum*), phacelia (*Phacelis distans*), and purple and white Chinese houses (*Collinsia heterophylla*). Stimulated to germinate by the fire's heat or contact with the charcoal of burned shrubs, the vigorous new fire community is nourished by minerals released to the soil by the blaze. Its days in the sun are short-lived, however. Within a few years after the fire, the shrub canopy of chaparral begins to close over the herbaceous plants, and soon virtually none remain. Their seeds, however, wait in the soil for the next fire.

L I F E U N D E R C O V E R

Fire gives new life to the chaparral shrubs as

well. Although some are consumed by the flames, others will survive. About half the species have specially adapted roots, or burls, that contain buds stimulated to grow when the top of the plant is injured. Some plants have these rejuvenating buds on their stems as well, and if they are not destroyed by the fire, they too will resprout.

Despite the fact that the tender and nutritious new stems are vulnerable to grazing animals,

within a year the former chaparral community is on its way to recovery. Within a few years, the shrubs will again close ranks and become impenetrable to humans. This dense canopy of twigs makes the chaparral an uninviting place, but a useful one. Chaparral protects watersheds on steep terrain, a crucial function demonstrated by flooding and massive soil erosion after chaparral is removed by fire or other means. Mature chaparral also provides protective cover for dozens of species of small mammals, birds, and reptiles that are easy prey on open ground.

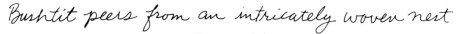
Bushtit peers from an intricately woven nest

A SURVEILLANCE SYSTEM FOR LYME DISEASE

The small brush rabbits that inhabit the chaparral in the Preserve are yielding clues about how long California has been home to *Borrelia burgdorferi*, the bacterium that causes Lyme disease (more correctly termed Lyme borreliosis). This tick-transmitted illness causes symptoms in humans ranging from headache and fever to arthritis and meningitis. *Borrelia* also produces a strong immune response in brush rabbits, which allowed biologists David Regnery from Stanford and Robert Lane from UC-Berkeley to conduct a retrospective study of the presence of *Borrelia burgdorferi* in natural environments.

From blood samples Regnery collected from Jasper Ridge brush rabbits between 1965 and 1972, he and Lane found that 16 of 18 animals had been infected with Lyme borreliosis. Their research is the first to suggest that *Borrelia* may have been in California for more than 20 years, well before the first human case of Lyme borreliosis in California was reported (1975) and even before the first human case was recognized in the United States (1969). This research demonstrates an important role of long-term studies: to provide baseline information in the reconstruction of phenomena such as the presence of borreliosis in California.

Rabbit
seeks safety
in the
underbrush

PLANT ADAPTATIONS

The many chemical compounds contained within the leaves and other organs of plants have a variety of functions, some of which are related to the plant's particular environment. For example, the sticky monkey flower (*Diplacus aurantiacus*) is a shrub that occurs at the edge of the hot, dry chaparral of the Preserve. Its leaves are coated with a resin that prevents excessive water loss and also filters potentially damaging ultraviolet light.

But the *Diplacus* leaves also face another threat — herbivory by insect larvae — and the plant's ability to deter herbivores depends on a variety of chemical compounds. The leaves' protein content determines their nutritive value to the larvae, so leaves are least susceptible to herbivores if they are protein-poor. However, the protein content also determines the plant's ability to photosynthesize and grow. The plant thus faces a trade-off between growth and susceptibility to herbivores. While studying this trade-off, biologist Hal Mooney developed a paradigm now widely used in understanding plant adaptations. He and collaborators have used economic models and cost-benefit analyses to evaluate how plants balance such trade-offs. In the case of *Diplacus*, they found it invests only moderately in leaf proteins and protects that investment with a chemical that deters leaf herbivory. The chemical it uses is the same resin that limits water loss and ultraviolet damage.

Sticky monkey flower

Stigma on the sticky monkey flower closes to trap pollen

Townsend's warbler

Lesser goldfinch takes cover in thistle

FIELD NOTE
DUSKY-FOOTED WOODRAT

While many animals that seek cover in the chaparral are content to make their nests in subterranean burrows or the branches of high trees, there is one mammal that prefers more architectural accommodations.

The dusky-footed woodrat (*Neotoma fuscipes*), a gray-brown, large-eyed rodent similar to the Old World rats in appearance, chooses to construct above-ground nests. These can reach 6 feet in height and several feet in width and are built of sticks, leaves, and snakeskins that the woodrat gathers from the scrubby underbrush. These structures have more than enough room for the hospitable woodrat, who measures less than a foot in length; as a result, the nests are also popular gathering spots for "guests" of other species: California mice, salamanders, and lizards.

Dusky-footed woodrat

Redwing blackbird perches atop the home of an industrious woodrat

Toyon and virgin's bower

Western bluebird

HERBS

Associated with the chaparral is another shrubby community of a very different nature. It is variously called "coastal scrub" or "soft chaparral." The member species are shorter than those of the chaparral, measuring less than 1 meter, and most have thinner leaves that drop during the drought rather than enduring it, probably because their shallower roots do not have access to water deep in the soil. The soft chaparral is found in rather dry coastal sites or within true chaparral as a successional community after a disturbance. Many species of the coastal scrub community such as California sage (*Artemisia californica*) and pitcher sage (*Lepechinia calycina*) are often highly aromatic, due to the terpenes they contain. These chemicals are a deterrence to many herbivores.

Coastal sage and chaparral have analogs in other parts of the world. For example, in southern France, an area that also has wet winters and dry summers, the chaparral equivalent is called the *maquis* and the coastal scrub equivalent is the *garrigue*. Although the species of these French communities are unrelated to their Californian counterparts, they are comparable in form and function. For example, the *garrigue* shrubs are similarly short and shallow-rooted, many having leaves that drop during drought. Many of these species are also rich in terpenes and provide the common cooking herbs sage, rosemary, and thyme.

The aromatic sage

78

Buck brush and California sage bloom on the hillside

Rattlesnake keeps cool in the shade of a rock

Sara orangetip butterfly

Holly-leaved cherry in full bloom

California quail

The dapper California quail, declared the California state bird in 1931, nests in the grasslands. The danger of this low vantage point is the loss of eggs to raiding carnivores.

Honey suckle berry

Redwood grove

THE SHELTERING GROVES

In cool, hushed groves of redwoods, broadleaf evergreen forests, and sun-warmed oak savannas, visitors to the Jasper Ridge Biological Preserve find shade beneath a rich and varied canopy of trees. These woodlands, containing many of the tree species most common to California, are sometimes whisper-quiet and sometimes raucous with the rush and chattering of birds and mammals that live and feed in their protective heights.

Most of the trees in the Jasper Ridge Biological Preserve are second growth, averaging some hundred years in age. Much of the original forests here were cleared more than a century ago by loggers or residents seeking firewood. Some of these second-generation trees belong to a species of mythic scale and antiquity, the coast redwoods (*Sequoia sempervirens*).

ANCIENT GIANTS

Found in the misty, coastal forests and steep mountain woodlands of California, these coast redwoods date back to the Tertiary period, millions of years ago, when the climate of the state was far warmer and wetter than today. Over the past century, logging has claimed much of the ancient, mature coastal redwood forests in the state. But not so very long ago, there were stands of redwoods in the Russian River valley that were thousands of years old. These trees had as many as 1.5 million board feet of standing wood per acre and were the tallest trees on earth.

Still, new redwoods readily sink their roots in California soil. On the Preserve, these towering trees are now found only in small stands on the moistest slopes. The young redwoods grow in rings, or "fairy circles," around their huge, now-vanished ancestors, some of which reached 100 feet in height and 20 feet in width. Nearby, in higher and cooler reaches of the Santa Cruz Mountains, the redwoods thrive in old and well-developed stands, once commercially logged and milled at the vanished town of Searsville.

Through the millenia, redwoods have held their ground in California despite the drying of the climate and the invasion of drought-adapted plants, such as oak and chaparral. They have survived because, to some degree, they are re-markably equipped to create their own moist and life-sustaining climate; twice as much precipita-tion falls under a redwood tree than falls in the

open. This is because redwoods can condense fog with their many small leaves and drip it to their roots. Since summer months are usually the fog-giest, this unique ability enables the redwoods to eliminate the dangerous effects of summer drought. In addition, the redwoods' dense canopy retains moisture for the plants by keeping the ground cool and reducing water loss from evaporation.

Another key to the redwoods' survival is their ability to withstand disaster. Their thick bark protects them from fire, and their tannin-filled leaves and wood make them virtually insect-proof. Moreover, if a redwood tree is injured, it is able to resprout from any part of its trunk.

Strangely, however, redwood trees do not reproduce from seed very successfully in a mature forest. In contrast to the large seeds of most forest plants, which are designed to support growing shoots for a long time under low-light conditions, redwood seeds are very small. Each year, a mature redwood will produce thousands of these seeds, but most will be lost to birds, animals, or fungi on the forest floor. As a result, it appears that the

Live oak was called 'encina' by Spanish explorers. An evergreen, it is found on the north-facing slopes of the Preserve, and has serrated, holly-like leaves.

redwood seed is most suited for germination in open sites, particulary in moist, mineral-rich soils.

LAND OF OAKS

Although it contains small areas of redwood forest, to a great extent the Jasper Ridge Biological Preserve lies firmly in the realm of the oaks. Oak woodlands cover most of California's coastal hills and valleys, and the Preserve is home to seven species of oak, including both deciduous and evergreen species and dozens of hybrids. The shrubby leather oak *(Quercus durata)*, whose strong and pliant branches were used by Native Americans for thongs, is found in abundance on serpentine soil. The majestic valley oak *(Quercus lobata)* offers islets of shade in the open grassland, while the deciduous black oak *(Quercus kelloggii)* is found in some of the Preserve's cooler habitats and higher elevations.

The two most abundant oaks on the Ridge are the California live oak *(Quercus agrifolia)* and the blue oak *(Quercus douglasii)*. The live oak, an evergreen, is found on the north-facing slopes of the Preserve in a community called the broadleaf

evergreen forest. It shares the forest floor with other dominant, large-leaved evergreens such as the fragrant California bay *(Umbellularia californica)* and the shaggy, red-barked madrone *(Arbutus menziesii)*. In somewhat wetter cli-

Blue oak

mates, this broadleaf evergreen community also includes the tan bark oak *(Lithocarpus densiflora)*.

The blue oak *(Quercus douglasii)*, which loses its leaves in fall, dominates the oak woodlands in drier sites near the crest of the Ridge, above the evergreen forest and just below the grassland. These oaks are home to a great diversity of birds, including the bushtit, chickadee, and titmouse. Their understory includes red-berried toyon shrubs and a variety of herbs and bulb plants that live beneath their protective canopy.

ROOTS OF SURVIVAL

Because many mature oaks are very deeply rooted trees, they have access to the water table as well as rainfall. When their acorns drop to the ground at the beginning of the rainy season in fall, the roots of the new seedlings grow down deep enough to reach a water supply that can last through the dry season. Shoots do not develop until spring, but the acorns contain energy-rich compounds to nourish the plant for this time.

Still, seedling mortality is high, especially in the first year when the roots have not yet reached the water table. Other causes of first-year mortality are predation on roots or shoots and injury. Root tips that are injured generate a new branched root, which can deflect the downward journey of the roots to the water source. Another cause of death is competition with other plants, a phenomenon particularly evident at the clear boundary of oak woodland and grassland. Oaks cannot successfully invade the grassland because the shallow-rooted grasses capture all the water from the upper levels of the soil in spring, giving oak seedlings little chance of surviving the ensuing summer months.

CIRCLE OF LIFE

Unlike groves of trees in more managed environments, the woodlands of the Jasper Ridge Biological Preserve are allowed to follow their natural life cycles without the interference of pesticides, tree trimming, and other maintenance activities. As trees in the Preserve die, the creatures that live or feed on dead or dying trees are allowed to flourish. Fungi, bark beetles, and other decomposers slowly return the dead plants to the soil, and small mammals and reptiles find shelter in the musty stumps and hollows.

Live oaks, basis of the food chain of the Costanoans

Sun seldom reaches
these north-facing
sandstone rocks
sheltered by a
canopy of live oaks

Beauty masks an oil that can be life-threatening

POISON OAK

What is the most abundant and hardy plant in the Jasper Ridge Biological Preserve? The answer may be poison oak (*Toxicodendron diversilobum*), whose oil causes an itchy red rash on human skin.

Poison oak grows as either a shrub or a vine. If the plant is growing near a tree, it develops as a vine and can grow as much as 100 feet in height. If no trees are near, it grows as a shrub. Small mammals such as wood rats find cover under poison oak shrubs, and in the grasslands, these shrubs can form islands 50 to 100 feet in diameter.

A California native plant, poison oak displays foliage of brilliant shades of gold, orange, and crimson in the autumn. Small and fragrant flowers blossom in late winter, and by summer's end, the female plants are covered with pearl-like clusters of seeds.

Poison oak's allergenic oil probably evolved as a defense against insects and viruses. It erupts on the surface when the plant has been bruised in some way and seals the rupture like a lacquer. The oil can remain active for an amazingly long time—as long as eight months—on clothing and other objects that it touches. If poison oak is burned, the oil can travel on the smoke and ash, and it can be life-threatening if inhaled or ingested. For the most part, however, poison oak does not seem to bother animals other than human beings. Deer enjoy the plant as food, and birds eat its seeds in fall.

Poison oak

FIELD NOTE
Oak Moths

Every five to seven years, the branches of evergreen oak trees on the Jasper Ridge Biological Preserve stand naked in winter as though they were winter-deciduous. The cause is a native herbivore, the California oak moth (*Phryganidia californica*), whose larvae specialize on oak leaves. Their feeding defoliates the evergreen live oak in late winter and the deciduous valley oak in summer. Few forest systems throughout the world experience such massive, cyclic defoliation.

It is remarkable that the oak moth larvae can find any sustenance at all in the tough, low-protein, high-tannin leaves. But their unusual diet preference plays a key role in the functioning of the oak woodland ecosystem. Many of the nutrients of the evergreen woodland are contained in the leaves of the trees. Because these high-tannin leaves are a poor food source for decomposers, they decay and return their nutrients to the forest very slowly. The oak moth larvae accelerate the recycling of these nutrients. Their feeding and digestion break down the leaves, and the chemicals contained in them, releasing nutrients in forms that can be used by many organisms.

Footbridge to the riparian woodlands

Nocturnal great horned owl awaits dusk to search for food

Mosses resist drought by absorbing water during heavy rains

Juvenile plain titmouse

FIELD NOTE
TITMOUSE, BUSHTIT, AND CHICKADEE

A prime example of the coexistence of different species of birds may be found in the blue oak woodlands of the Preserve. As many as 40 bird species may be seen darting about among the short, thick branches of the blue oak trees, and 25 species have been known to nest there.

Clear differences in the way these birds seek food, nest, and define their territory allow them to share the woodland resources without obvious competition. For example, if you observe an oak tree early in the morning, you may find a plain titmouse, a bushtit, and a chestnut-backed chickadee together in its branches. If you watch them closely, you may also find that they are each eating insects from a different part of the tree.

You may see the bushtit taking insects from small twigs of the oak, the titmouse probing the bark of large branches, and the chickadee doing a little of both. These evolved behaviors reduce direct competition for food and may be the principal reason that these three species coexist in the same woodland.

Chestnut-backed chickadee

Black oak comes into leaf

Indian warrior is found only under oaks, upon whose roots it is semi-parasitic

The sheltered environment of the Jasper Ridge Biological Preserve protects its native populations of plants, animals, and insects from many of the effects of increasing urbanization. But the Preserve faced a novel threat in the summer of 1981, when several local counties instituted a program of aerial pesticide spraying designed to eradicate the Mediterranean fruit fly ("medfly") that would have doused the Preserve with malathion-laced protein bait.

Researchers and University administrators successfully mobilized to safeguard the Preserve. While surrounding areas were showered 12 to 24 times with malathion, the Preserve was officially exempted and became the only control site within the medfly spray zone. With the Preserve as a control site, long-term comparisons of the sprayed and unsprayed areas have been possible.

Les Ehler, an entomologist from UC-Davis, discovered that during and after the spray period, the Preserve's populations of gall midges (*Rhopalomyia californica*) were low and stable, while in local areas sprayed 24 times, a tremendous increase in the number of midges occurred. There, the pesticide had unleashed the gall midge from its natural controls by poisoning wasps that parasitize the midges. Conditions elsewhere suggested that this midge outbreak could have been prevented; there was no significant increase in midges just south of the Preserve in areas that had received 12 sprayings,

suggesting that the degree of environmental disruption was related to the number of dousings. In spite of precautions to spare the Preserve, there were some effects of the spraying. Spray drifting into the Preserve along its boundaries may have affected animals moving between protected and unprotected areas. For example, before the medfly eradication program, bats were commonly seen after dusk in the Preserve. For some years after the spraying, they were rarely seen.

gall midge

Buckeye renewal

The fruit of the buckeye is poisonous

Winter fog
lends eerie
cast to
lattice of
valley oaks

Farewell-to-spring, a California native

Acorn woodpecker adds to a communal food supply

The delicate mariposa lily belies a deceitful trap

Early morning on the grassland

Leather oak acorns

Alders send a tangle of roots in search of water

Frosted lupine

Big-leaved maple with flowers

Leatherwood, a flowering shrub, has no petals

Few irises grow on the Preserve

Valley oaks are embraced by morning fog

White fairy lanterns are also called satin bells

Mist rises from Searsville Lake

WETLANDS
WORLDS ON WATER

On mornings in early spring, the rising sun breaks up the dark green shadows on Searsville Lake, shattering the surface with shards of light. Coots squawk and blue-billed ruddy ducks coast and bob in rippling rings. Pied-billed grebes chatter, and cattails rustle in the breeze. Life in the wetlands awakes.

The waters of Westridge, Corte Madera, Sausal, and Alembique creeks all gather into Searsville Lake in the Jasper Ridge Biological Preserve. First dammed in 1892, the lake once covered 90 acres in a Y shape, with arms reaching through swamp and marshlands. Today, the swamp is drying out, and the lake itself covers less than 23 acres. More than 45 feet of silt has gathered on the bottom, reducing the lake's depth to only 22 feet at the center. Still, despite its diminishing volume, the lake is home to a rich array of plants and animals.

PLENTIFUL AND VARIOUS

Freshwater clams and crayfish are abundant, and for many years local residents regularly fished the lake for its stock of large mouth bass. Green sunfish, black crappies, bluegills, brown bullhead, and mosquitofish are found in the lake. Foothill yellow- and red-legged frogs live secretly along its edges, and western pond turtles scuttle slowly through the marshes. Western terrestrial and aquatic garter snakes slide along the lakeshore, and bats feed nocturnally on insects hovering above the water.

Black double-crested cormorants

Birds throng about the lake. Egrets and blue herons live and fish there in numbers, and flocks of red-wing blackbirds chase would-be invaders from their lakeside territories. Local and migratory ducks abound, from the green-winged teal to the canvasback and the northern shoveler. Loons and tundra swans appear occasionally upon the water, and double-crested cormorants dry and preen themselves on shore.

The lake is also rich in aquatic plants, from the floating American water fern *(Azolla filiculoides)* to yellow-flowered *Jussiaea*, of the evening primrose family, in the shallows. Yellow iris *(Iris pseudacorus)*, an Old World native often grown as an ornamental, has spread along the margins of the lake for at least 20 years.

Floating parrot feather (*Myriophyllum*) was introduced into the lake some years ago and it is now so dense in some shallow parts that mosquitofish cannot penetrate it to eat mosquito larvae. An underwater mower keeps the parrot feather and mosquito population in check.

BEYOND THE LAKE

The wetlands of the Preserve encompass not just the lake but also moist soil in swamps, marshes, streams, and pools. The once-verdant wetland below the dam along San Francisquito Creek is now usually dry in summer. As late as 1912, the creek flowed year-round as far east as El Camino Real. A section of both banks of San Francisquito

Creek lie within the Preserve, and here one finds isolated second-generation stands of towering coast redwood. Other common woody species along the creek banks include the yellow-flowering box elder *(Acer negundo)* and big-leaved maple *(Acer macrophyllum)*, willows of several species *(Salix)*, white alder *(Alnus rhombifolia)*, California bay *(Umbellularia californica)*, and California hazelnut *(Corylus californica)*.

In their shadows creep orange California newts and small-headed black salamanders. Bullfrogs bellow after nightfall, and raccoons "wash" their meals of nuts and insects in pools of water. Walking in the riparian (streamside) woodland, one also finds the ubiquitous poison oak *(Toxicodendron diversilobum)* and occasional pawnbroker bush *(Eunonymus occidentalis)*. Creek dogwood *(Cornus californica)*, western leatherwood *(Dirca occidentalis)*, and California live oak *(Quercus agrifolia)* thrive in the moist creekside environment, as do herbaceous flowering plants, including the only population of tiger lily *(Lilium pardalinum)* in the Preserve. This species is now quite rare in the Santa Cruz Mountains, since people have gathered its bulbs for generations. Scarlet monkey flower *(Mimulus cardinalis)*, a perennial, is also found occasionally in the creek bed.

Rich in plant and animal life, the fate of the wetlands of the Jasper Ridge Biological Preserve is far from clear. Their future depends, in part, on whether the lake will be permitted to silt up naturally, in which case it will evolve eventually into a meadow, or whether it will be preserved as a reservoir by dredging. That is a difficult choice facing biologists who study the Preserve and its complex ecosystems.

Great blue heron

Cattails trap silt
in the shallows
of the lake

One of several species of cattails found in the sandy shallows of the lake. Cattails begin to fill in marshy areas as the lake succession continues its natural course from reservoir to meadow.

Ring-necked ducks are annual winter visitors

Dry cattails along the lake

FIELD NOTE
CALIFORNIA NEWTS

When winter rains start to fall, the dark-brown, yellow-bellied California newts begin their reproductive journey from their feeding grounds to the streams, ponds, or lakes where they were spawned. Navigating by unknown means, the newts travel by the hundreds across the rough terrain of the Preserve back to their birthplaces to spawn, a distance of as much as four miles away. The trek can take five months. They recognize their breeding places by chemical senses, then mate and lay

California newts return to their birthplace to

their eggs in water. Along their journey, the California newts help protect themselves from predators by secreting a poisonous chemical onto their skins. They feed on earthworms, snails, slugs, sowbugs, and other insects, gulping down their prey whole. This difficult pilgrimage takes place annually during each newt's life, which may last as long as 21 years.

Spawn

The journey begins

Forster's tern

Winter rains inundate San Francisquito Creek

Pied-billed grebe

THINK GLOBALLY, MEASURE LOCALLY

The sediments of Searsville Lake are inhabited by organisms that affect not only the chemistry of the lake but of the atmosphere as well. In the oxygen-poor lake bottom, decomposers break down plant and animal material; this decomposition releases methane gas that bubbles to the surface. When methane reaches the atmosphere, it acts as a greenhouse gas, trapping heat near the surface of the earth. Together with other greenhouse gases such as carbon dioxide, methane concentrations in the earth's atmosphere are increasing at rates that have led scientists to predict a warming of the globe during the next century.

When researchers Laurence Miller and Ronald Oremland of the U.S. Geological Survey measured methane production by Searsville Lake, they found that it releases methane at rates comparable to cypress swamps and other freshwater swamps. These rates are higher than rates observed by the researchers in saline lakes such as Mono Lake, but lower than those associated with human activities such as rice cultivation, municipal landfills, or cattle breeding.

Thus, Searsville Lake, the only freshwater lake in central California managed primarily for research, has provided critical data for estimating global methane production by natural freshwater habitats.

Parrot feather mat protects mosquito larvae

FIELD NOTE

MOWING THE LAKE

Parrot feather *(Myriophyllum)*, named for the feathery appearance of its leaves, is an aquatic plant that thrives in the warm, shallow marshland of Searsville. It was introduced into the lake decades ago.

In summer and fall, parrot feather becomes a green mat so thick that ducks walk across it. The ubiquity of this plant has contributed to unusually large numbers of mosquitoes in the area. Mosquitoes lay their eggs on the surface of the parrot feather mat. The leaves of the parrot feather screen out mosquitofish, the major predator of the larvae, so that when the larvae hatch, they feed undisturbed. Thus, a substantial number of them survive to adulthood.

To control the mosquito population, the parrot feather is mowed with mechanical cutters mounted on barges. This provides the mosquitofish with large open areas and access to the larvae. Mowing is considered just a temporary solution,

however—parrot feather propagates by cuttings, and residue from mowing spreads the plant even more widely. Long-term, direct solutions to mosquito population problem must be devised.

Currently, the lake is a test site for various ecologically sound methods of directly controlling the mosquito population, such as introduction of nematodes (larvae-eating worms) and the use of insect growth regulators.

Tracks along the the sandy lake shore show the path of the nocturnal raccoon. Perhaps the raccoon has "washed" its food there; scientists now believe that these mammals wet their food not to clean it but because their salivary glands provide inadequate moisture.

Evidence of a raccoon's evening raid

Fall

Afternoon at Searsville Lake

Snowy egret

Banana slug

Eocene rock along San Francisquito creek, Sculpted by rushing water

Wood Duck

Year-round

residents,

wood ducks on

Searsville Lake

nest in the

hollows of nearby

trees. When the

young are ready

for their first

outing, they jump

from their nest

and bounce on

the ground

unhurt. The

parents then herd

them to the water

for a swim.

Crayfish

Solomon's seal is a denizen of the redwood forest

Tart wild blackberries are plentiful on the Preserve

Willows and alders in fall colors ring the lake

Early winter sunset over Scarsville Lake

The interaction of lichen and host is complex

A LEGACY TO SAFEGUARD

The wetlands, groves, and rolling grasslands of the Jasper Ridge Biological Preserve offer quiet riches for the eye, the mind, and the spirit. For many, they are a tranquil respite from the press of urban or academic pressures. And they are a living laboratory in which scientists can study, over decades, the way a butterfly species interacts with its environment, or the way a native grass responds to different soils and climates. But for other visitors, attracted to the Preserve's near-wild environments, they offer a chance merely to notice what is usually rushed past and never seen: the colorful markings of a mariposa lily, the leap of a black-tailed jackrabbit, or the white cheeks of a ruddy duck as it skims the surface of the lake.

But in this age of increasing development and environmental risk, the Jasper Ridge Biological Preserve offers something even more important: a chance to safeguard some of the plants and wildlife that belong to California. The Preserve encompasses nearly every plant community of central and coastal California, and it contains a biotic richness that has become rarer and more precious with time.

Some 748 kinds of mammals, fish, reptiles, amphibians, and birds, and 5143 plants are native to California. Nearly 900 of those species are rare, threatened, or endangered, or risk becoming so. As new residents stream into California at the rate of some 600,000 per year, new homes and businesses will continue to crowd and endanger the fragile habitats of native plants and wildlife. Much is at stake. In the past century, the extinction rate of the world's species has increased nearly 400-fold.

Jasper Ridge is one of the few protected places left near urban areas where native species can live unthreatened by development or well-intentioned interference. Since 1848, development has claimed an astonishing 80 percent of California's coastal wetlands, 89 percent of its riparian woodlands, 94 percent of its interior woodlands, and 99 percent of valley grasslands. But behind the gates of the Preserve, moles tunnel freely, wild cherries bloom, and black-tailed deer seek sanctuary under the shady oaks.

Science benefits, and so do we all. By setting aside this 1200-acre "island" of California, we have been able to uncover pieces of our natural and historic past. And we are gaining understanding and safeguarding some of its riches for the future.

Fern creates a delicate lacework extending from the rock

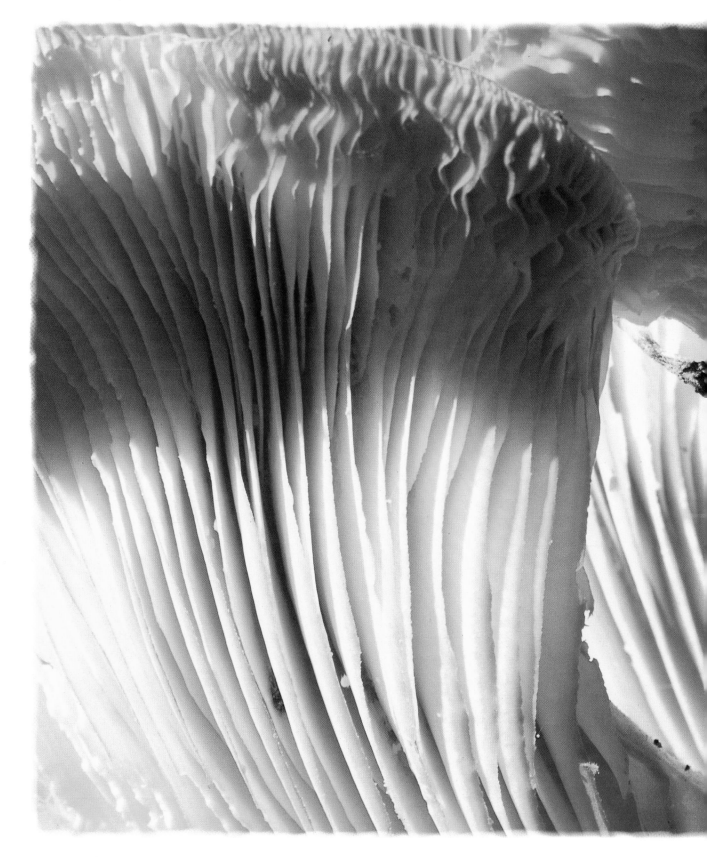

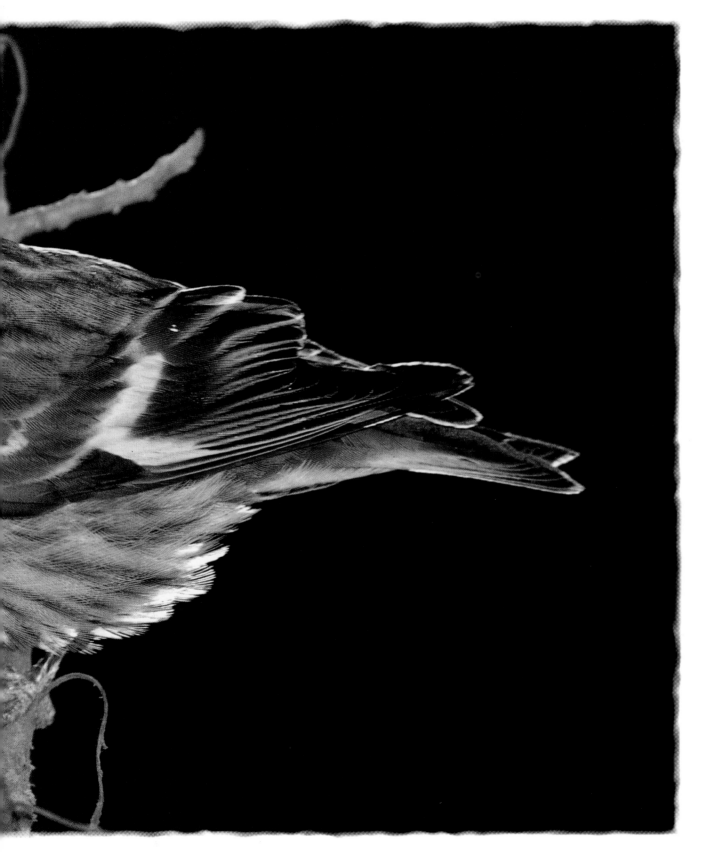

Floral beauty larger than life

AUTHORS AND PHOTOGRAPHERS

THE AUTHORS

Barbara Bocek is the university archaeologist and manages the University's archaeological resources, consisting of 56 significant prehistoric sites. She is also a lecturer in the Department of Anthropology. Dr. Bocek received a BS degree from the University of Oregon and an MA and PhD in archaeology from Stanford University. She has done field research at Willamette Valley prehistoric sites, excavations of cave and rockshelter sites in Peru, and investigations of Jasper Ridge, Stanford West, and other sites along San Francisquito Creek. Dr. Bocek has received fellowships for her studies from the Smithsonian Institution, the Andrew Mellon Foundation, and the National Science Foundation. She is a member of the Archaeological Resources Task Force and Costanoan Advisory Committee for the County of Santa Clara.

Nona Chiariello has been the scientific coordinator of the Jasper Ridge Biological Preserve since 1985. She holds a BA degree from Swarthmore College and a PhD from Stanford University; she conducted her PhD research on the serpentine grassland at Jasper Ridge from 1976-81 with Harold Mooney as her advisor. Dr. Chiariello was an assistant professor at the University of Utah for three years before returning to Stanford. She is the only scientist stationed on the Preserve; she coordinates the use of the Preserve by as many as 30 researchers each year and continues her own research on the serpentine grasslands.

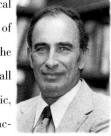

Paul Ehrlich, Bing Professor of Biological Sciences, received an AB from University of Pennsylvania and an MA and PhD from the University of Kansas. He has travelled to all continents, from the arctic to the antarctic, establishing research sites to study the interaction of ecology, evolutionary biology, and behavior. Dr. Ehrlich has conducted research on a wide array of biological problems ranging from the dynamics and genetics of insect populations to experimental studies of the effects of crowding on human beings. He and his wife, Ann, work collaboratively on policy research in human ecology. Dr. Ehrlich is the author of more than 500 scientific papers and articles and 30 books, including *The Population Bomb*, *The Machinery of Nature*, *New World/New Mind*, and, most recently, *The Population Explosion*. He is the honorary president of Zero Population Growth, president of the American

Institute of Biological Sciences, a fellow of both the American Philosophical Society and the American Academy of Arts and Sciences, and a member of the National Academy of Sciences. He has received awards from the American Association for the Advancement of Science and the Royal Swedish Academy. Additionally, Dr. Ehrlich is a correspondent for NBC-TV.

 HAROLD A. MOONEY, professor of biological sciences, has played a central role in developing the field of plant physiological ecology. After completing his undergraduate education at UC-Santa Barbara, Dr. Mooney received a PhD from Duke University. He served on the faculty at UCLA before joining Stanford's Department of Biological Sciences in 1968. He is currently carrying out research on plant adaptation with an emphasis on costs, benefits, and tradeoffs of various plant traits. He is also involved in research on the effects of global change on ecosystem function. Dr. Mooney is on the editorial boards of a number of scientific journals including *BioScience, Oecologia,* and *American Naturalist.* He was elected to the National Academy of Sciences in 1982, and received a Merit Award from the Biological Society of America in 1983. He is a Guggenheim and Alexander von Humboldt fellow, a member of the American Academy of Arts and Sciences, and is the president of the Ecological Society of America.

 JOHN H. THOMAS received his BS degree from the California Institute of Technology and his AM and PhD from Stanford University. He is currently a professor of biological sciences at Stanford and curator of botany at the California Academy of Sciences. Dr. Thomas is also the director of Stanford's Dudley Herbarium. The Herbarium contains more than 850,000 specimens of dried plants; it was founded in 1891 by Professor William Russel Dudley, the first professor of systematic botany at Stanford, and was named for Dudley after his death in 1911. Thomas' research interests include the flora of western North America, botanical history, conservation, and herbarium management. Author of numerous publications, his *Flora of the Santa Cruz Mountains* has been widely used since its publication in 1961.

PETER M. VITOUSEK is professor of biological sciences and scientific director of the Jasper Ridge Biological Preserve. He received his BA from Amherst College and his PhD from Dartmouth College. He has been at Stanford since 1984. Dr. Vitousek has served on the  editorial boards of various scientific journals including *American Naturalist, Ecological Society of America,* and *Annual Review of Ecology and Systematics.* His research interests include the effects of exotic species on the ecosystems of Hawaii and California and the effects of tropical deforestation on the atmosphere.

THE PHOTOGRAPHERS

CHARLES COMFORT received an MD from Stanford Medical School in 1960 and practiced psychiatry in Palo Alto until his death in 1986. He took photography as seriously as his medical practice and co-owned a gallery in town called the New Roses. His photographs, some of them dating from the 1950s, are valuable documentary evidence of the changes that have occurred at the Jasper Ridge Biological Preserve.

PETER LATOURRETTE is a consultant in microwave component design and software development when not in service as a nature photographer. He received a BSEE, MSEE, and Degree of Engineer from Stanford University. Mr. LaTourrette was invited to Jasper Ridge Biological Preserve in 1986 to record the rare sighting of the red-naped sapsucker and Lewis' woodpecker. When he realized that the Jasper Ridge slide file was nearly devoid of bird photos taken on-site, he spent the next three years exhaustively photographing the Preserve's winged creatures. Mr. LaTourrette, whose work has appeared in national journals, has photographed birds all over the world; his current project involves photographing endangered species in the Hawaiian forests.

JOEL SIMON received his first camera as a birthday gift when he was 6; his first nature photographs were shot that same day and featured a caterpillar that he chased around the yard. Mr. Simon received a BA, BS, and MS from Stanford University, and he worked as a product designer before joining the Stanford Alumni Association Travel Study staff in 1980 as photojournalist and aquatics director. Mr. Simon is a licensed scuba instructor and has taught college-accredited courses on marine biology in the U.S. Virgin Islands. His photography has been featured in the *Stanford Magazine* and in various travel and photography publications.

Alder roots reach for a drink

JASPER RIDGE BIOLOGICAL PRESERVE
STAFF

Scientific Director: Peter Vitousek

Administrative Director: Alan Grundmann

Program Coordinator: Monika Björkman

Teaching Assistant: Tim Hullar

DOCENTS

Jim Allen	Toni Corelli	Margaret Green	Leonard Rush
Christine Andrews	Mabel Crittenden	Marye Harding	Elizabeth Rush
Bob Augsburger	Betsy Crowder	Reed Hastings	Steve Schlozman
Jane F. Becker-Haven	Rigdon Currie	Joe Herzog	Bob Shelby
Monika Björkman	Marge De Staebler	Mary Hufty	Lynn Tennefoss
Irene Brown	Fran Delagi	Debi Jamison	Victor Thompson
Robert Buell	Janet Doell	Lalu Kiesling	Sara Timby
Gene Bulf	Linda Elkind	Bill Kirsher	Pete van Heyst
Ruth Buneman	Molly Engelbrecht	Ann Lambrecht	Bob Ward
Brenda Butner	Ron Fark	Jean Lane	Cindy Wilber
Jack Chin	Joan Fearing	Winkie Lennihan	Ellie Wood
Jean Clark	Louise Fletcher	Patti Poindexter	Woody Woodward
Bill Clark	Ed Fryer	Ruth Porter	John Working
Betsy Clebsch	Timmy Gallagher	Alice Reeves	Sunia Yang
Bob Collyer	Lindy Gardiner	Lennie Roberts	Carol Zabel
Polly Cooperrider	Carol Graham	Anne M. Rosenthal	

STUDENTS

James Alborough	Suresh Jesuthasan
Kevin Ascher	John Keller
Heidi Ballard	Flora Lu
Pam Briskman	Michael Margolis
Steven Chui	Dave Mellinger
Jackie Collier	Lara Mendel
Marc Duaphiné	Liz Moyer
Brendan Del Favero	Julie Radoslovich
Geoff Engman	Danny Sigman
Becky Fennerty	Kiran Soma
Mary Gehan	Edith Struik
Calvin Goforth	Diane Sweeney
Nick Haddad	Jeff Tumlin
Sharon Hall	Marc Whitley
Christy Halvorson	Tammy Wallace
Cyndi Holtz	Julie Willard
Drew Hudnut	Bradley A. Zlotnick
Tim Hullar	

A future contained within this fragile shell

ACKNOWLEDGMENTS

Jasper Ridge: A Stanford Sanctuary has been made possible through the generous support of the following individuals and corporate sponsors:

BENEFACTORS

Ronald B. Arps

Peter & Helen Bing

Laura & Edward Birss

Lawrence & Ruth Chu

Edwin Bingham Copeland '95

Louise M. Davies

Mr. & Mrs. Reid W. Dennis

Mr. & Mrs. William S. Floyd

Robert Charles Friese

Robert M. Golden

Rufus C. Goodwin, MD '40

Robert E. Hungate

Jim & Mary Bee Johnston

Carolyn King

Jean & Bill Lane

Joan & Mel Lane

George E. McCown

Mr. & Mrs. Charles T. Munger

Margaret K. Schink

John D. Weeden

PATRONS

Frederick Bold, Jr.

Books On Tape Inc.

Mr. & Mrs. Thomas H. Broadus

Richard F. Cahill

Edith Lang Duncan

Molly Hurlbut Engelbrecht

Barbara Sanborn Flannes

Mary C.J. Goni

Ruth & Alfred Heller

Phyllis & Robert Henigson

Leo Holub

Dorothy Collom Horstman

Kartozian Family Foundation

Will W. Kelly

Jeanne & Bill Landreth

Elizabeth I. McCormick

For Jim & Dorothy McLachlan

Lynn & Leslie Pasahow

Greg & Dion Peterson

Mr. & Mrs. Thomas P. Pike

Heather A. & William A. Sampson II

C. Raymond Schatz

Mrs. Robert Lee Sims

Transamerica Corporation

Lois & Jim Ukropina

Carrie van Heyst

Mrs. Alexander von Hafften

Betty Jo & Hal Williams

Roy & Betty Vitousek

SPONSORS

Mr. & Mrs. William H. Abbott

Jeanne Falk Adams

Marian Menninger Adams

Dr. Daniel S. Alegria

Pattie & Harlan Amstutz

David H. Anderson

Elisabeth K. Anderson, MD

George D. & Norma Anderson

Gina Anson

Joan & Paul Armer

Frank H. Armstrong

In Memory of Helen W. Arndt

Claudia & Dixon Arnett

Richard K. Arnold

Temple W. Ashbrook II

Doug & Karen Atwood

Robert Augsburger

Virginia Nunan Axenfield

Owen, Molly, Katie, & Austin B.

Ross Bagdasarian

Marjorie K. Balazs

Isaac & Janine Barchas

Dennis & France Bark

Eunice F. Barkell

Robert & Peggy Barmeyer

Lorrie Van Rie Barnes

Stanley M. Barnes

Victoria Mae Barry

Philip C. Bartlett, MD

Jeanne & Ken Bauer

Alfred X. Baxter

W. Reese Baxter, MD

Gerry Morgan Bayuk

Irene Beardsley & Dan Bloomberg

Helen Sweeny Beardsworth

Betty Scattergood Becker

Janice Becker

Hal Bender

Pat Benefiel

Alice R. Berry

Barbara T. Bilson-Woodruff

W. Richard Bingham

Monika Björkman

Mark Willis Blackman

R.C. Block

Sharon G. Boots, PhD

James C. Bottomley

Gray Boyce & Tom Bliska

William E. Boyd

Mr. & Mrs. Brenton Bradford

Dr. Gregg Everett Brandow

Mr. James B. Brennock

Karen Coley Bridger

H. William. & Diane J. Bridgford

Carol K. Brittain

Kilbee Cormack Brittain

The Brose Company

Mr. & Mrs. James L. Browne

Phyllis M. Browning

Joe H. Brumbaugh

Richard I. Buckwalter

Jean & Robert Buell

Vic Buffalow

Ravi A. Bulchandani

Mark D. Bullock

Edward Ramsey Bunting

Jefferson Burch

In Memory of L.L. Burlingame

Rae Burns & Robert Kanne

George L. Burtness

Arthur G. Burton

George L. Burtness

Betye Monell Burton

Brook Byers

Mariann Byerwalter

Bruce Cabral & Kimberly Harney

J. Emott Caldwell

John N. Callander

Mr. & Mrs. Donald A. Campbell

Mrs. Lindsay Campbell

Barbara Anne Carey

Karen Booth Carlson

Honora & Bob Carson

Barbara Castagnoli

Thomas Castle & Pamela Howard

Robert & Shirley Cavigli

Mrs. John M. Cazier

Alan & Coeta Chambers

Stan & Carol Chapman

John G. Chapple, MD

Chung-I. Wang Chiang, MD

Margaret C.W. Chiang

Doug & Gail Cheeseman

Jack Chin

David Jordan Clark

Dr. & Mrs. William H. Clark

Anthony Paul Clevenger, PhD

Russell Clough

J.H. Cochran, Jr., MD

R. Frank Coltart, Jr.

Betty & John Colwell

William & Kathy Connell

Tita Cooley

The Corelli Family

Harry J. Cornbleet

Constance Crawford

Irene M. Creps

Dr. Nancy Jewell Cross

Elizabeth Blair Crossman

Betsy Crowder

Rigdon Currie

Bradley James Dary

Brian William Dary

Dorothee Diebel Dary

Leonard James Dary

Tom & Ann DeFilipps

Susan Dauphiné & Marc Dauphiné

Velma A. Denning

Mr. Chester W. Dennis

Palmer & Cort de Peyster

Dick, Sylvia, & Nicholas DeVeaux

Dominic & Cynthia DiSalvo

L. Robert Dodge

Oliver S. Dominick

Yvonne Carlier Donahue

The John Dowdell Family

Mr. & Mrs. Philip G. Duffy

Ann A. Duwe

Martha N. Eakland

Bert T. Edwards

Marie Babare Edwards

Freda Francke Eisenson

Dr. & Mrs. Gilbert Elian

In Memory of Betty Elliott

Suzanne Berger Erikson

Chuck & Sheri Evans

James Fagan, BA '49, JD '54

Mr. Theodore A. Falasco

Craig & Sally Falkenhagen

In Memory of Flora May Fearing

Bruce & Elissa Feldmeyer

Noel & Sally Fenton

Bob & Susan Fiddaman

Barbara Denning Finberg

Victor J. Fish, MD

Dr. & Mrs. J. Peter Fitzpatrick

Richmond Flatland, Jr.

Camille K. Fong

Dr. & Mrs. Max Forbert

Christopher G. Foster

Florian & Katherine Frank

T. David & Anna Horton Freeman

Geoffrey & Dorothy Fricker

Ayisha Lee Fryer

Alison Clark Fuller

Jack & Janwyn Funamura

Ed Furukawa

Arnold D. Gale, MD '71

Mr. & Mrs. Douglas S. Gamble

Richard Garlinghouse

In Memory of Charlene Garry

Jessica & Gabrielle Garton

Mr. Ronald Brown Garver

Howard Stiles Gates

Larry Geisse

Sandra L. Genis

Candace L. Gietzen

Brooks Gifford, Jr. '58

Laurie Gill

Ann Witter Gillette

T. K. & Beth Gilliam

The Earl Goddard Family

Marcus L. Godfrey, Jr.

John D. Goheen

Rufus C. Goodwin, MD '40

Robert R. Graham

Carmel L. Granger

Ralph H. Grebmeier

Peter & Patty Gregg

Mr. & Mrs. Alan Grundmann

Liane S. Guild

Richard R. Gunter

Mr. & Mrs. Carroll M. Haeske

Ruth & Ben Hammett

Mary M. Handelin

Eric J. Hardgrave

William O. Harrison, MD

Molly Haselhorst

Colleen M. Hayden

Walter & Kay Hays

Barbara Ann Theis Hazlett

Duane & Margo Heath

Eleanor A. Hedenkamp

William G. Heitner

Gladys Medalie Heldman

R. A. Helliwell

In Fond Memory of Rae F. Helmke '29

Mr. & Mrs. John Hessel

Victor L. Hetzel '32

Jo Carol Gordon Hiatt, MD

Jonathan R. Hiatt, MD

Marianne N. Hill

Ken Himes

Evan Eades Hodder

John E. Hoegg

Leo & Helga Hoenighausen

George & Ann Hogle

Mr. & Mrs. Robin Hood

Mr. & Mrs. Albert J. Horn

Tracy F. Hunt

Mr. & Mrs. James R. Hutter

Martin W. Irwin

C. Ray Jackson

Pauline M. Jackson, MD

Chris Jaenike

Pat Janney

Anne & Doug Jensen

Eleanor Jernigan

Clark & Janet Johnson

John & Phyllis Johnson

Dr. & Mrs. Robert S. Johnson

Richard & Caye Johnson

Ruth & Chet Johnson

Jackiel W. Joseph

Elizabeth M. Kennedy

Dr. H. Parley Kilburn

George P. & Margaret R. Kimball

Dennis B. & Suzanne B. King

Martha E. King

Eric A. Kirianoff

Mr. & Mrs. Philip M. Klauber

Kneedler & Sanson Families

James Shingle Koford

Ralph & Margie Koldinger

Hunt Kooiker, MD, MPH

Krogh Pump Company

Ruth & Rex Kramer

Charlie Kuffner

Mark L. Labowe, MD

Peter Lacy & Janice Cowen

Edward B. Landels

Ron & Judy Lange

Roger Lawler

David & Jean Laws

Henry M. Layne

Elizabeth LeCount

Esther M. Lederberg

The Letendre Family

Peggy Moore Lewis

Francis V. Lloyd, Jr.

Bob & Kathy Logan

Julie & Noel Longuemare

Pauline Lord

Paul V. Lorton '31

Carol Lovell & Kenneth Hynes

Gary C. Lucich

Elsa Widenmann Ludwig

Luigi Luzzatti

R.W. Lyman

Maria T. Mackel

Marta Perry Mackenzie

Alan H. MacPherson

George & Marjorie Mader

Anne & Lynne Manrique

Mr. & Mrs. Andrew T. Marcopulos

Mr. & Mrs. Theodore A. Marcopulos

Charles D. Marple, MD

George L. Matthaei

Mary Ann Corthell Matthews

Arthur Matula

Eleanor R. McCalla

Margaret Robison McCarty

Perry & Martha McCarty

Charles E. McClung

Beverly McClure

Garth McCune

Lester S. McElwain

Kevin Michael McFarland

James & Sara McManis

Lynda A. McNeive

Mr. Robert W. Medearis

Ben Harris Meisel '93

Michael Bernd Melnick

Ed Mendell

Robert Mendez

Charles & Nancy Merrill

Philip E. Merritt

Robin S. Midkiff

M. Ronald Miller

Mr. & Mrs. Bruce T. Mitchell

Lloyd A. (McDonnell) Mitchell

Mr. Owens Minton

Charles J. & Lin Morehouse

David F. Morgan

Richard B. Morrall

Charles N. Moss, MD, DrPH

Sharryn Mounts

Daniel & Virginia Murphy

In Memory of Murphy

Dr. & Mrs. James P. Nash

Carl & Elizabeth Naumann

Patricia Lynch Needleman

Cliff & Pat Nelson

Jeffrey A. & Margot P. Nelson

Walter Edward Nelson

Robert M. & Mary W. Newell

Ellen & Walter Newman

Dr. & Mrs. Walter F. Nichols

Mrs. Jean L. Nilsson

William & Virginia Notz

George & Carla Nowell

Eileen M. Oakley

Barbara O'Brien

John D. & Lois W. O'Brien

Dr. & Mrs. Floyd Okada

Stephen Otto

Joan R. Palmer

Mary Patrice Pang

The Parmer Family

Susan Passovoy

Douglas S. Patton, MD

Harold E. Pearson

D. Buttner WoodSpell Peckham

Donald A. Pepper

Laura Klauber Peterhans

Kirk L. Peterson, MD

Richard Philippi '34

David A. Pierce

Cima & Muriel Pollia

Paul & Katherine Ponganis

Mr. & Mrs. Gordon L. Poole

Ruth & David Porter

Richard Pospisil Family

Oser Franklin Price

Bruce M. Putnam

Helen & Dan Quinn

Ann Elizabeth Rafferty

Steven B. Raffin, MD

Berta & Gail Rathbun

Dr. & Mrs. Allen K. Ream

Dr. Jerome & Ruth Reed

Monique M. Regard, MD

Joan Reinhart

Walter B. Reinhold

Mr. & Mrs. William B. Renton

Jenifer A. Renzel

Gary & Angela Retelny

Elizabeth V. Reynolds

Mr. Jonathan C. Rice

John & Joy Richards

Jon Karl Riordan

Mr. & Mrs. Rodger Rickard

Jim & Sandi Risser

RNS Mechanical Inc.

John & Alison Roberts

Dr. & Mrs. Ernest Rogers

Helen Fuller Rohrer

Beth & Peter Rosenthal

Nancy G. Rosenthal

Alice & Bill Rosenzweig

Clara Belle S. Ross

Fred Ross

Ulla & Harvey Rothschild

Don H. & Carole L. Rowe

David & Marilyn Rumelhart

Dr. John C. Russell

Robert E. Saak

Steve & Zoe Salter

Letty McCaskill Sample

Abram & Dorothy Sangrey

Mr. & Mrs. Wm. W. Saunders

Alice & Stan Schlichting

Patricia & Earl Schmidt

In Memory of Peter J. Schmidt

David & DeeDee Schurman

Marc I. Schwarzman '76

Carlton E. Schwerdt

Mary Carroll W. Scott

Laura Jane Seery

Robert Setrakian

Carolyn & Don Shaw

Patrick A. Shea

Hazel Sheets

Chris C. Shulenberger

Leonard J. Shustek

Harriet Theis Sidone

Charla Gibson Silverman

Mr. & Mrs. Daniel A. Sisk

Dr. & Mrs. John P. Slater

Mrs. Dan Throop Smith

Justin G. Smith

R. Lawrence Snideman II

Wilson & Susan So

Peter & James Solt

Jean Staver Somer

Suzanne Chute Spaulding

Virginia Spears

Mrs. Milton H. Sperling

Ralph Joshua Spiegl

Stephen R. Staub

William C. Stein

Joanne Stenger, MD

Ellie & John Stern

Elizabeth Stevenson

John & Marilyn Stevenson, Jr.

Louise Stewart

William R. Stobie, Jr.

James Stockton '55

Daniel E. Stone

Mr. Andrew Ross Wald

Debbie Duncan & Bill Stone

Jennifer, Allison, & Molly

Martha June Lewis Strauss

Charles Edward Street III

Mary K. Sullivan

Joy Olsen Surbey

Wm. John Sweeney

To Honor Patricia J. Sweeny

Ana Yelena Sycip

Raymond J. Szczesny

Laurence Munroe Taber

Keith Tao, MD

Julie & Hoff Stauffer

Dorcas H. Thille

Joan Seavey Thomas

Anita & George Thompson

James W. Thornton

Mary Alice Thornton

Nathan A. Tiner, PhD

Geoffrey Tompkins, MD

Carol Mixter Tormey

Eugene T. Turley

Arleen Tweedy

Mr. & Mrs. Burton J. Twitchell

Gretchen & Robert Tyler

James Morgan Upton

Arvid Underman, MD

Albert & Antonia Van Horn

Marjorie Petersen Varner

George & Barbara Vendelin

Robert & Winnifred Verbica

Peter & Suzanne Voll

Virginia Walbot

Mr. Andrew Ross Wald

Scott & Barbara Wallace

Annabelle Joan Ward

Bob & Connie Ward

Dr. Linda Shipley Warren '80

Bleecker & Helen Wass

J. Michael Watt

Jay Michael Watt, MD

Mrs. Ralph Wardlaw Watt

Robert & Linda Petty Weed

Alan N. Weeden

David B. Weissman

Phyllis Wells

Mr. & Mrs. William P. Wentworth

Gary Joseph Wenzel

William C. Weyher

Dr. Harry L. & Cathy White

Mrs. Arlington C. White

Wallace Whittier Family

Mrs. Blake C. Wilbur

C. Eskola Williamson, MD

John & Virginia Williamson

Helen & Lauress Wise

Bev & William Wohlfort

In Honor of Bernard M. Wolfe

Miriam E. Wolff

Woodside Trail Club

Dr. & Mrs. S. C. Woodward

James M. Woolfenden

John & Beverly Working

Ellen & Tom Wyman

Yogi Bear & Ritcas

Robert G. Younge

Rosalie V. Zari

Caroline A. Zimmerman

Bradley A. Zlotnick

CREDITS

EDITOR-IN-CHIEF
Della van Heyst

MANAGING EDITOR
Nora Sweeny

DESIGNER
Tom Lewis

ART DIRECTORS
Cynthia Sardo
Sam Lewis

ART PRODUCTION MANAGER
Nancy Cash

ILLUSTRATIONS AND CALLIGRAPHY
Roger Chandler

PHOTOGRAPHY
Charles Comfort: *iv-v, vi-vii, viii-ix, x-xi, xii-xiii, xvi, xxii, xxvi, 23, 25, 31, 32, 34, 38-39, 43, 47, 49, 50, 51, 53, 58, 61, 65, 71, 75, 76, 80-81, 83, 85, 89, 91, 92-93, 94, 97, 102, 106, 108-109, 110, 112, 113, 114, 116, 117, 118, 119, 120, 121, 122, 126-127, 133, 136, 139, 143, 145, 146, 147, 148, 150, 154-155, 158-159, 160-161, 164, 168, 170*
Peter LaTourrette: *xxv, 37, 42, 45, 57, 66, 67, 68-69, 72, 73, 77, 82, 84, 98, 100, 101, 111, 124, 125, 128, 132, 134, 138, 140, 141, 144, 156-157, 162-163*
Joel Simon: *ii-iii, xxi, 11, 13, 16, 20, 22, 24, 28-29, 30, 35, 46, 54, 55, 59, 62, 79, 86, 99, 103, 107, 115, 129, 130-131, 142, 149, 153*
Department of Special Collections, Stanford University Libraries: *5*
Stanford University Archives: *6, 7, 8, 9, 19, 27*
News and Publication Service, Stanford University: *165(P.E.), 166(H.A.M.)*
Nona Chiariello: *105, 137*
Keith Comfort: *36, 60, 167(C.C.)*
John Boykin: *166(J.H.T.)*
Rod Searcy: *165(B.B., N.C.), 166(P.M.V.), 167(P.L., J.S.)*
Paul Ehrlich: *41*

SPECIAL THANKS TO the Centennial Operating Committee, the School of Humanities and Sciences, Stephen Peeps, Ewart Thomas, William E. Stone, Alan Grundmann, Monika Björkman, Margaret J. Kimball and the staff of the Stanford University Archives, Irene Brown, Elizabeth Geismar, Amy Pilkington, J. Christopher Cunningham, John Boykin, Elena Reese, Martin Lytton, and Priscilla Murray.

Woodside

GOLF COURSE

JUNIPERO

ACCELERATOR

SERRA

280

ROAD

LINEAR

Zoology Cabin

Rattlesnake Rock

Indian Mortar

Hillside Laboratory

Stanford

San Francisquito

Bartholomew Exclosure

Shack Riders Clubhouse

Searsville Dam

Searsville Laboratory

Former Bathhouse

Searsville Historical Marker

Main Gate

Frasier Beach

Town of Searsville

Jasper Ridge

Searsville Lake

Webb Ranch

Vestal Exclosure

Weather Station

Creek

Hermits Cabin

Highest Point in Preserve

Hermits Mine

Causeway

San Andreas Zone

PORTOLA

SAUSAL

Valley

MAPACHE

Corte

CRESTRIDGE

DRIVE

RIDGE

EL C...

DRIVE

WHISKEY HILL

Bear

MANZANITA

CAÑADA